nico
the end

james young

THE OVERLOOK PRESS
WOODSTOCK · NEW YORK

First published in 1993 by
The Overlook Press
Lewis Hollow Road
Woodstock, New York 12498

Library of Congress Cataloging-in-Publication Data

  Young, James (James Edward), 1952-
  Nico : the end / James Young.
    p. cm.
    1. Nico, 1944-1988. 2. Singers-Biography. 3. Rock musicians-
-biography. I.. Title.

ML420.N615Y7 1993
782.42166'092 —dc20
[B]
ISBN: 0-87951-504-X   93-26188
                                            CIP
                                            MN

First Edition

CONTENTS

CONTENTS

PREFACE

Nico

The Grünewald-Forst cemetery is situated on the outskirts of Berlin, by the Wannsee Lake. In twentieth-century consciousness Berlin has been synonymous with a kind of claustrophobic angst, a landlocked Madagascar of bizarre hybrids. So it's strange that Nico should be buried in a pretty, almost rural setting, within the perimeters of a city renowned for its monsters, but one for which she no longer felt much affinity.

Like many of her generation, born shortly before or during the war, she felt, at best, an unease towards her country and its guilty past. She no longer saw herself as specifically German. She spoke in English. She dreamt in English. She sang, mostly, in English. And although it saddened her to see the country divided geographically and politically, she never liked to stay there very long. Now she's a permanent resident.

From the start, Nico seemed destined for a life of strange tensions and weird scenes. Her father came from a rich background, her mother from a humble one. Needless to say, his family deemed it an unsuitable match. Nico was born Christa Paffgen in Cologne on October 16, 1938. Her father insisted on her being brought up a Catholic, with all the attendant mysteries and miseries.

When the war began, Nico's father was conscripted. He was apparently a poor soldier, unable to respond with convincing obedience to the military and ideological discipline of the Third

Reich. In 1943 Nico's mother received a letter informing her that he'd been wounded in the head and had been taken to a military hospital. His injury resulted in brain damage, and he had become subject to bouts of insanity. The Nazi authorities had one simple, expedient solution for the treatment of the mentally ill – extermination.

Nico and her mother then moved to Berlin to stay with her aunt, but the Allied bombing was so intense they sought refuge with Nico's grandfather, a railway man, in Lubbenau – about ninety kilometres east of Berlin. There Nico would play with her cousin in the local graveyard and watch the trains (those trains?) go by. At night she could see the burning red sky of Berlin in the distance.

After the war they returned to the city, her mother making her living as a tailor, dressing her daughter as finely as she could. She was a beautiful child and her mother was anxious that she should always look her best. Nico disdained the rigours of conventional German education, and at the age of fifteen, with the encouragement of Ostergaard, a Berlin couturier, she left school to become a professional model. Initially her mother was reluctant to allow it, but Ostergaard managed to persuade the doubtful parent, and by the age of seventeen Nico had become the best model in Berlin. Then, inevitably, she went to Paris, where she worked for, among others, Coco Chanel, who took a personal interest in her androgynous protegée.

To further her career, and to escape Chanel's attentions, she went to New York to work for Eileen Ford. There, energised by the city and liberal amounts of amphetamine ('They used to give it us so we'd stay thin'), she earned $100 a day, enough to buy the house in Ibiza that became her European base for the next decade. It was in Ibiza that she became 'Nico' – taking the name from a photographer friend in memory of his ex-boyfriend.

Nico moved from scene to scene. In Rome she became involved with the Cinecittà set and found herself conscripted into Fellini's *La Dolce Vita*. It was a walk-on part that became extended into a definite role, due to the director's fascination with her phantom-like presence on the set. Not much real acting ability was demanded of her, more the skills of the catwalk. Fellini, though, was keen to develop her and use her for more pictures, but he became irritated by her habitual laziness. When she failed, after repeated warnings, to make an early morning camera-call, he fired her.

She pursued the idea of becoming an actress a while longer, taking part in Lee Strasberg's Method classes in New York. Later she would claim that she had been in the same class as Marilyn Monroe.

Then came the music scene. Initially it involved a lot of hanging out. She took lessons in narcissism from Brian Jones of the Rolling Stones. He loved those Germanic blondes (though her hair was bleached and her blood mixed). Arm-in-arm they would pose for the adoring crowds at the Monterey Pop Festival or float regally down the King's Road, King and Queen of the carnival. At this time she cut her first record, a Gordon Lightfoot song called 'I'm Not Saying', instantly forgettable, and also had her first meeting with her future mentor – Andy Warhol. He had just dropped in on Swinging London en route to New York after a holiday in North Africa sampling the tight delights of Moroccan youth.

In 1965 she did a spell as a cocktail singer at the Blue Angel Lounge on East 55th Street and soon found herself in the company of Bob Dylan. At that time the scene was divided between the Dylan camp – straight – and the Warhol camp – camp. Nico's temperament was more suited to Dylan's circle, she loved the man and his work, but Dylan's romantic attention was engaged elsewhere and there would be no real place for her except as an acolyte.

Warhol, on the other hand, had found a group at the Café Bizarre, playing curiously titled songs like 'Heroin' and 'Venus in Furs'. The Velvet Underground. Warhol decided that Nico should become their figurehead, much to the reluctance of the rest of the group, Lou Reed and John Cale in particular. Still, they acceded to their patron's demands – new instruments, free rehearsal space, food, drink, drugs, instant chic, in exchange for letting Nico do a couple of numbers. Nevertheless they delighted in giving her a bad time, bullying her into singing their way – which depended upon whatever caprice the drugs dictated. They'd torment her with tricks like switching off her microphone, or blasting her out with guitar noise – anything to make her feel more paranoid. Paranoia was the dominant theme of the Factory floor.

Lou Reed wrote a few tunes for her, which they got her to sing in that bleached, throwaway style — 'All Tomorrow's Parties', 'Femme Fatale', 'I'll Be Your Mirror' — but there was always a problem about who was doing what. Nico was not an instrumentalist, and therefore couldn't reintegrate with the rest of the group once her songs were over. Besides, Lou Reed was the leader, he wrote most of the material, he was the real singer.

'Lou never really liked me,' she once told me, 'because of what my people did to his people.'

The truth was perhaps more banal – he resented being upstaged by her.

Although they only sold a modest amount of records in their time, the Velvet Underground exerted a potent influence and found their true apotheosis in the 1980s. They were perfectly in tune with the dominant themes of the decade – cynicism, careerism, amorality.

With the encouragement of Jim Morrison, amongst others, Nico went on to become a solo artist, accompanying herself on harmonium and reverting to her real singing style – dark, European and deeply melancholic. John Cale, though antagonistic to her as a member of the Velvets, produced her best work: *Marble Index*; *Desert Shore*; *The End*; *Camera Obscura* – the last with myself as arranger.

She was never better than when sitting alone at her harmonium, singing one of her disturbing little songs with its hints of folk melody, German *Ländler* and Bach chorales – all in a voice so unbelievably deep it bordered on Wagnerian parody. There were times, intermittent to be sure, when even the most blasé of audiences, saturated with the gimmickry of the modern pop spectacle, were held in its dark embrace.

The scenes shifted – initially according to the dictates of her career, latterly according to the demands of her heroin addiction. In the early eighties there had been a huge influx into

Britain of high-grade heroin from Iran. (Heroin is a useful commodity in times of political turmoil – five times the value of gold.) For a junkie Britain was the place to be, and Nico found herself a niche in Manchester, where there was, and still is, a thriving drug and music scene.

Nico was not a pop star. 'Famous, not popular,' was how one Japanese promoter described her. In fact, she wasn't even that famous. She never made much money as a singer, and what little she did make she spent immediately. She didn't own a house or a car or a TV or even a single copy of one of her own records. She had a handful of friends who would visit her occasionally with cakes and biscuits, and a few crumbs of gossip that would sustain her interest for a little while before you sensed your presence was no longer necessary.

It was a way of life she'd followed since she was a teenager, a life without any of the more familiar creature comforts that people acquire to fend off boredom and loneliness. The Chanel suits she'd been given in her days as a *Vogue* model had long since been jettisoned in favour of the more androgynous black trousers and jacket. Her heroin addiction had, at one time, provided some sort of psychic refuge – filling her days with the traditional junkie routine of trying to score – the inexorable search for a good connection.

But even these squalid adventures began to lose their special *frisson*; towards the end of her life, she turned her back on the drug that had become synonymous with her name and persona. Or she simply ran out of veins.

I first met Nico in November 1981 in a now-defunct Oxford nightclub, playing to an audience of amphetamined undergraduates hyped-up on the Velvet Underground myth and enjoying their brief fling with Bohemian lowlife before taking up their careers in advertising. She seemed both amused and bemused by her celebrity. Once again the promiscuous attentions of the pop world had settled upon her, identifying her as the precursor to a tortured nihilism then fashionable amongst the young.

In the cramped dressing-room, while poetically thin young

men hung upon her every word and Nico lookalikes with pale lipstick stared relentlessly at their 'Warhol superstar', hoping to discern the secrets of her charisma, she rummaged through her cavernous shoulder bag with increasing desperation. The little wrapper of heroin she'd spent so much of the day trying to obtain had disappeared.

She cursed herself for being so careless, becoming more and more frantic in her search. She would have to perform without the confidence the drug gave her. As she rose to go to the stage, I spotted the small white envelope beneath her chair and handed it to her, thus sealing the bond of a working relationship that was to last the rest of her life.

Nico kept on working because she had to. There was her habit to maintain, a permanent drain on her resources. Thousands of pounds were shot away on colossal binges, so that she'd end up after a three-month tour as broke as she'd begun it. This didn't seem to disconcert her, though – something would always turn up. She believed that fate, or some unforeseen coincidence of events, would rescue her from disaster at the last minute. Sometimes it did, but increasingly she came up against a more cynical response to her predicament. Her spiritual origins were in the Beatnik subculture of the fifties and the narcotic euphoria of the sixties. But the wild party was long since over and, in the cold light of the hard-bitten eighties, people were less inclined to offer the few remaining stragglers a lift home.

That she was a monster became apparent to all those who were with her for any length of time. She was a dreadful cadge, and her gratitude was so transparently insincere that it was almost endearing.

I knew her only in the last decade of her life, long after the credits came up. She had exhausted most people's patience or interest. What might have been the forgivable narcissism of a fashionable beauty had now become a tiresome and undignified egoism. After all, she was no longer charming or mysterious, what right then had she to tantrums or impatience? Her features, riven by years of narcotic abuse, bore little trace of the 'icy Germanic beauty' that has been chronicled so meticulously at the court of the Great Wigola. The 'dark Teutonic soul' that had once added such a puzzling bitterness to the sickly sweet froth of pop seemed to have become an absurd caricature of nihilism, a genuine emptiness.

She seemed as if blown away by it all . . . The relentless pressure to stay cool, to allow the will of others, in the shape of the lens, to penetrate and push her towards her own annihilation. There's a Warhol/Morrissey film called *Chelsea Girls* whose leitmotif is a broken sequence of Nico crying, really crying. About what, who knows. But the pain is visceral, the tears are real. It's an art-house animal experiment. Method: give her all the stuff she wants, and slip in something new, untried, untested. Context: private loft preview for the Artocracy. Result: a Modern Morality Play. Chastening.

The people who gravitated towards Nico were generally those on the margins of polite rock'n'roll society. It sounds quaint now – given the age of the medium, its vast corporate identity, its entrenched conservatism – but there was a time when rock music embodied some sort of threat, or if not that, at least a kind of freshness and spontaneity. Perhaps Nico represented a bit of that lost world of recklessness, of extremes.

We were all peripheral people . . . peripheral to her, just as she had been peripheral to the world that had made her and later eclipsed her in terms of wealth and celebrity. We worked in an environment into which no respectable A&R man would enter, places in which the strung-out or the lonely would go to console themselves, in the company of one who seemed to embody their alienation.

All of this was far, far away from Warholian glamour, with its surface glitter of camp self-effacement and its chilling undertow of ruthless self-interest. No longer a Factory factotum, Nico nevertheless retained a certain loyalty towards her one-time mentor.

'Andy always seems too busy to see me when I call him,' she complained.

'That's probably because you keep asking him for money,' I offered, knowing full well, as perhaps she did, that she'd long since outlived her use to him. Her beauty faded, her celebrity marginalised, she'd lost her iconographic value as an image of the 'European Moon Goddess', once so essential an acquisition to the great collector's gallery of social archetypes.

Into this void I stumbled. Although I'd fiddled around with groups in my teens in Manchester, I'd been to college, got myself a degree, and was about to start on a Master of Philosophy course at Oxford. I had some months to go before my course began, and I was mooching around for something to do that was unrelated to academic work. I'd been practising at my piano, perhaps in the hope of finding bar work, maybe abroad, when an old school-friend looked me up, a certain Dr Demetrius.

Dr Demetrius

He wasn't a doctor, nor was his real name Demetrius. He had a whole string of pseudonyms and aliases. He insisted it gave his life a 'poetic mystery' – it also left a false trail for hungry creditors. We'd known each other since childhood in Manchester. He'd always had a gang around him; he'd always derived his greatest satisfaction from pulling people of disparate backgrounds into his circle. Demetrius had been working as a promoter on the Manchester New Wave scene since the late seventies and he'd put Nico on at one of his venues. He'd introduced us when she came to Oxford a couple of months earlier and I'd mentioned to him that if ever she needed a piano player, I'd be grateful if she'd give me a try-out, as I liked her stuff. He'd called me to say she was putting a group together for a tour of Italy . . . why didn't I come up to Manchester, get better acquainted?

What follows is the story of Nico's last 'scene' – the whole scene, the weird little universe she inhabited in the middle of nowhere and of which she was the fixed centre. The characters who orbited around her – the has-beens, the could-have-beens, the never-will-bes – are people whose lives are rarely sung in the deafening hyperbole of Rock History. We weren't especially

gifted, or at least our talents were rarely exploited to the full –
aesthetic concerns being invariably subsumed beneath the more
urgent need to score heroin. However, we did have one thing in
common . . . Nico.

She influenced us all. It may sound absurd but, despite the
monstrous egotism and the sordid scenes, there was something
almost *pure* about her. A kind of concentrated will. Not pretty,
sweet or socially acceptable, certainly, but intense, uncom-
promising and disarmingly frank. She influenced us, perhaps
indirectly . . . none of us wanted to *be* like her, selfish and
ungracious, but she helped us map out a different landscape to
our lives – different to the prevailing eighties one of getting-
onism. We never, for an instant, thought of ourselves as part of
the Music Business. We were just there when it didn't happen.

AQUAVILLE

'Libraries are where you go when you're afraid of your dreams.'

You can't get up to much in a library. They're like monasteries but with the whispered torture of a thousand rustling nylons. SILENCE must be observed at all times, yet distractions are infinite as every train of thought is derailed by boredom or lust or the soft, over-ripe thud of bulging briefcases yielding their dead weight of learning; the screams of chairs dragged to favoured corners; and always the breathy flutter of the turning page.

It was November 1981 and I was going insane – though, as this was Oxford, very discreetly – when a familiar rotund figure stood at the top of the steps to my flat, blocking out the daylight. I hadn't seen him in five years, since when he'd put on an extra few stone, lost his hair, and awarded himself a doctorate.

'Looks like I beat you to it, old boy,' said Dr Demetrius in a mock Oxford accent as if he was still continuing some running argument, some unresolved rivalry from half a decade before.

Then the deepest female voice I'd ever heard, wearing a German accent as heavy as a leather Gestapo coat and louder than the foghorn on the Bismarck, boomed round the corner.

'Where are yoooo?'

'Neek . . . Neek . . .' shouted Demetrius. 'Come and meet my old friend Jim, or rather "James" as I believe it is now.'

'Hey-lloo.' There was a rather heavy-set woman of about

forty staring through and beyond me and into the flat next door, with strange blue/grey eyes that were striated with red veins, like a map of Hell.

'May I use your bathroom?'

I was a creature who scratched his dry claws about the catalogue room – what was this?

'First on the left.' I pointed. When she'd gone I asked Demetrius who she was.

'Nico, the singer. You know, "Nico" – from the Velvet Underground.'

'Oh . . .' I had a sudden flash of some bad time when I was about sixteen . . . a girl grieving over some other guy who'd taken her innocence – someone older, smarter, more experienced, more mature. Now I remembered, Nico accompanied tears and sexual guilt. Music for a torn hymen.

'She looks a bit the worse for wear,' I said.

'She needs a fix, old man,' replied Demetrius.

'In my bathroom?'

'These are desperate times,' he said.

Suddenly I had a famous junkie in my house. I was in a rush. I'd left my books in the library. Junkies and famous people demand extra attention, like children. I wasn't ready for the responsibility.

'I must get back . . .'

'Don't you want to come with us?' asked Demetrius. Nico was playing at Scamps Disco, above Sainsbury's in the Westgate Shopping Centre.

'I don't think so. It's the noise . . . the crowds . . . I prefer the library. Libraries are where you go when you're afraid of other people,' I said.

'My friend.' Demetrius put his hand on my shoulder. 'You've spent too much time alone with books . . . libraries are where you go when you're afraid of your dreams.'

For five years I had heard nothing of Demetrius, ever since we rented a run-down semi back in Manchester, and now here he was on my doorstep, unannounced, with a sixties icon in tow. Since we'd last seen each other Demetrius had been house manager of a punk club, running around the Manchester 'scene' in an ever-expanding suit until he was big enough to have the door held open for him at High & Mighty. Nico had arrived at just the right time. She was in need of a good manager, one who shared the same sophisticated cultural background, a man of subtlety and learning . . . 'Dr' Demetrius was born.

Manchester: February 1982

The taxi pulled into a quiet suburban cul-de-sac on the southern edge of the city. Once comfortably affluent, now a little run-down. The people next door ran a kebab van.

I rang the bell . . .

. . . and waited.

'Hey-lloooo?' There was that voice again, heavy with the whole weight of her being. 'Who *is* it?'

'It's James . . . Jim . . . the piano player?'

The door opened.

She looked puzzled. Then, slowly, a twitch of recognition crawled across her face. She smiled, sort of.

'Oh . . . yeees . . . sure . . . I guess you'd better come in.'

I followed her down the hallway into the back room. The curtains were closed. Everything had collapsed to floor level: cushions, TV, blankets. A gas fire wheezed on the wall. Below it, staring fixedly at the ceiling, lay a young man, a kid really. All he had on was a pair of Y-fronts and a ripped T-shirt . . . I waited in the doorway. Was this a sex thing?

She went over to him and crouched by his side, fiddling around under some cushions, finally retrieving a hypodermic needle she'd secreted in haste. She held it point upwards and depressed the stopper. Then, quickly and without a word, she jabbed it into the kid's leg, pulling back the plunger, filling up the syringe.

Silently I sidestepped into the kitchen. It was cold, clean and pristine – no one had ever cooked a meal in there. There was a pan on the stove, half full of reddish water. The fridge was empty except for half a lemon. I found a full packet of tea in the cupboard, a fancy blend from Fortnum & Mason. I looked for the teapot. There wasn't one. That's why there was still plenty of tea. These were people who would never think of buying a teapot.

'Hi . . .' She was at the door. I jumped, embarrassed at being caught poking around.

'Sorry . . . as you can see, we have nothing. We're sta-arv-ing.'

Every word stretched and pulled. Every syllable weighed and counted. Gravitas, or emptiness?

'Did you get here OK?'

'Yes . . . there's a through train.' I glanced at the pan of bloody water. 'Your friend . . . is he all right?'

'He's sick . . . he has an aaabscess . . . dirty needles. I have to syringe it out . . . disgusting, no?' She laughed. 'That's how we are, us wicked people.' The half smile flickered again, briefly. 'Do *you* think we're wicked?'

'Yes.' I offered her a cigarette. '*Very* wicked.'

'Now I remember. You're the one who found my stuff that time in Ox-foord.' There was an emphasis on the 'foord'. 'Jesus, if I had it now . . . I hoped it might be someone else at the door.'

'Thanks.'

She nodded in the direction of the other room: 'I can't be expected to take care of everyone . . . I've only one shot left. I guess that's the test, huh?'

'The test?'

'You know – if you re-e-ally care for someone then you'll share your last shot with them. No?'

'I dunno . . . I've never been in that position.'

She looked me up and down. She saw baggy trousers, sensible shoes. I saw black leather and motorbike boots.

'You mean,' she continued, surprised, 'you've never been in lo-o-ve?'

'No, I've never used a needle. The thought of it . . . I get nauseous . . .'

I guessed that for her there wasn't much left to talk about. She changed the topic from drugs to money and started wringing her hands, pacing up and down.

'I have no money . . . *nothing*. The landlord asks for the
rent all the time but I told him, I'm a reclo-o-ose, I bother no
one!' She wrung her hands again. 'Do you have £20 you could
lend me until I see Demetrius?'

'Where *is* Demetrius?' I asked, hoping to sidetrack her.

'He always seems to be eating,' she said, a mixture of
anger and disappointment in her voice. She stepped a little
closer. I could smell heavy perfume and something strange and
sickly underneath. 'What about the boy?' she whispered.
'What can *I* do? I can barely keep myself . . . I'm not his
mother.'

'I'm sure Demetrius will think of something.'

Dr Demetrius had plenty of ideas and could make things
happen. He also had £20.

The rehearsal was set for 3.00 p.m. at Echo's. He was the
bass player. We'd met each other before, occasionally, in
darkened rooms. He lived in the heart of Prestwich, the quiet
Jewish part of north Manchester. Tall, Victorian Gothic
houses where the sun never shone. Engels had lived round
the corner, writing by gaslight, and Demetrius took us to
see his place on the way. The roof was gone, the windows
smashed in – skinned and gutted, it just needed one of those
ravenous winds off the moors to devour it completely. A
Chinese delegation stood outside, querulous . . . No shrine
to the people here. Not even a plaque. They kept checking
their mysterious guidebooks, perhaps to see if they'd got the
right address.

'Right address,' said Demetrius as we drove past, 'wrong
philosophy.'

Echo's place was a little more intact than Friedrich's . . . but
only a little. Children were playing in the garden. Three of
them, all girls. They had strange, evocative names, Justine,
Sadie, Mercy. Inside, the house was very Catholic: bleeding
hearts that glowed in the dark; sacred hearts in blue and white
satin with silver lettering; burning hearts whose flames of
martyrdom flickered and spiralled; hearts with arrows; hearts

with thorns; red hearts; black hearts. Enough to give the Jewish neighbours heart-failure.

Echo

Echo was small, made of wire and rags, just turned thirty. He wore a fedora hat and had bad teeth from too much amphetamine, but he was attractive in a way unique to the debauched. Beneath the haggard exterior lay a truly wasted interior. You knew he was consistent all the way through and could always be trusted to see the worst side of bad luck. He also spoke with a consistent softness, so that you'd have to ask him to repeat everything. You'd strain to catch the gist of what he was saying as the words surfaced in a tortured whisper from his tar-blackened lungs and his nicotine-lined throat and out through gaps in his crumbling teeth. It flattered you into thinking that only the wise could hear and it enabled him to retread a twisted path through his own Vale of Tears.

His cigarettes were the cheapest brand, No. 6, sold in tens. His match broke as he tried to light one. 'Tour of *Italy*'s OK but I'd prefer to be where it's safe an' warm an' nothin' changes.'

'Is there such a place outside of the womb?' I asked.

'Yeh,' he croaked, finally lighting his dimp. 'Nico's 'andbag.'

(Deep in the ambiotic still of Nico's bag a small blue notebook sucks its thumb and awaits the desperate delivery of a dealer's address.)

Demetrius left the artists alone, in Echo's parlour, to wrestle with the Infinite; driving off in his sagging old Citroën Pallas in search of a phone. He never felt at ease unless there was a phone within reach and Echo's place had few direct connections with the outside world. Even the entrance was a secret, tucked away at the side, past a barricade of dustbins and rusting prams.

'Purra brew on, pet.' Echo's wife vanished obediently into the kitchen to make tea. (Once you get north of Hampstead, the sexual territories become more clearly defined.) Faith was even thinner than Echo and deeper into denial and repentance, if that was possible. She had shining red hair down to her waist that her children would take turns to comb. Faith was the perfect weeping Magdalene for Echo's domestic Calvary.

Nico and Echo (Necho) sat together on the sofa, facing the fire.

''Ow're yer fixed, sweet'eart?'

'I'm down to my cottons,' she replied glumly.

'Give us twenny an' I'll pop round the corner.'

She handed him £20 that Demetrius had just 'loaned' her.

'I'll come with you . . . d'you have – er – something sharp?'

'Here you are.' I pulled out my Swiss Army knife.

She looked at me, stupefied.

'Come on,' said Echo, 'it's a kosher gaff. We'll be all right.'

He took her by the arm. As they were going out, I heard her say, 'He's a bit of a klutz, that Jim.'

'Nah,' said Echo, ''e's just a grammar-school boy, out of 'is depth.'

I stared at the children's goldfish. We commiserated blankly with each other. The Three Graces danced and sang among the yew trees and rhododendrons.

> Hark! Hark!
> The dogs do bark,
> The beggars are coming to town;
> One in rags,
> One in jags,
> And one in a velvet gown.

Beyond the garden was an empty church that marked the dividing line between the Torah and the Gospels. Echo would go sketching up there among the gravestones. He was a good artist, but indiscreet enough to let Faith see a nude portrait of his mistress . . . all curves, roundness and fertility. He just couldn't resist showing it to visitors. It was his first wholly successful piece and he was proud of it. He tried to bluff Faith that it was a pure product of the imagination. She averted her gaze every time she walked past, as it hung there above the fireplace, Venus Triumphant.

'What d'yer reckon, Jim?' he'd croak time and again.

'Pretty good,' I'd say.

'She dunt much care fer the ol' jigga-jigga, but she can suck a bowlin' ball through a Lucerzade straw.'

He insisted it was an arrangement they both preferred, as 'Left Footers'. Sex was best expressed with the least physicality. The conventional sex act could be messy and unprofitable, fraught with sudden embarrassments and disclosures. It was enough for him to have a pair of crimson lips around the tip of his being. Why be beastly? And what did Venus get? . . . Immortality.

Toby

Toby, the drummer, lifted the gate latch. Immediately the children fluttered around him, pulling at his cap, tugging at the sleeves of his leather jacket. They adored him. Everyone did. Tall, amiable, curly-haired, he had that perennial boyishness that girls especially find so attractive and unthreatening. (Though he could pack a punch, he preferred to take it out on his drums.)

I let him in.

'Hiya, Jim, what's er . . .' He looked around. 'Who's er . . . where's er . . . ?'

I shrugged my shoulders and mimed a shot in the arm.

He nodded, flipped open his Bensons, threw me one, and settled into the *Daily Mirror*.

'Know 'ow many dates we're doin'?' he asked, snorting a line of bathtub speed.

'All I know is, it's two weeks in Italy, the Dr Demetrius sunshine break.'

He offered me the rolled £5 note. I shook my head. He snorted the other line.

'Wur is 'e then, physician ter the famous?'

'Gone to find a phone. He's trying to locate someone called Raincoat.'

'Raincoat?'

'Yes. I'm sure that was his name . . . the sound engineer.'

Toby laughed. 'I know Raincoat . . . "sound engineer" is it now? Last week 'e wur a ladies' 'airdresser.' He carried on laughing until he began to cough up his smoker's phlegm, which he spat out the window.

> ('One in rags,
> And one in jags . . .')

'Toby . . . Toby,' waved the children.

After an hour of chainsmoking smalltalk we decided it might be a good idea if we at least set up the instruments.

The rehearsal room was, in effect, Echo's spare bedroom, a place to hide from conjugal demands or excited children. Heaps of gutted speaker cabinets were piled up like empty coffins, guitars with no strings, blown-out amplifiers. In the corner, by the window, was Echo's bed. And on the bed, arranged in a sculptural contrapposto, were Nico, and Echo, fast asleep, a hypodermic at their side. Despite their narcosis there was something innocent about them. They recalled one of those seventeenth-century marmoreal effigies of dead infants embracing . . . skin an alabaster white, heads thrown back in a lifeless surrender to the Eternal.

'That's me off.' Toby fixed the brim of his cap, buttoned up his jacket and was out the back door. I followed him.

Demetrius was in a parenthesis of bliss, sitting in his car, listening to country and western and chewing on a Big Mac.

Toby tapped on the window:

'It's not 'appenin', mate . . . Scagged up.'

Dr Demetrius kept an office on the top floor of a crumbling but dignified Victorian block on Newton Street, near Piccadilly, in the centre of Manchester. Brooding nineteenth-century warehouses, empty then, at times of use to the Jewish and Asian wholesale garment trade.

A pickled old Irish misanthrope ran the lift:

'Woy don't yer fockin' *walk* up, y'idle swines?'

Toby and I stood there, speechless.

Demetrius butted in: 'Good afternoon, Tommy, top floor, toute suite, last one up is a Proddy dog.'

Old Tommy wheezed whiskey-stained threats under his breath as he cranked down the ancient brass handle. 'Headen . . . Godless, idle headen.'

As we stepped out he coughed up a crescendo of bronchitic malevolence. 'Fock-ock-ockin' Fairies . . . should be strangulated at birth.' The lift door slammed and he descended back to his cubbyhole in hell, waiting for someone else to hate.

'Do step this way, gentlemen.' Demetrius ushered us into the nerve centre of his entertainment empire. He lifted a stack of invitations to Dr Demetrius's CREDITORS MEETING AND ANNUAL BALL off one chair and brushed a cat off another.

'Take a pew.'

I sat down and looked around.

Paperwork was strewn everywhere, heaps of unopened bills in the In tray. On the wall above his desk hung a photo of Carl Gustav Jung and another of Will Hay, the comedian, in his phony headmaster rig.

Dr Demetrius spoke with a pronounced Manchester accent which he tried to submerge beneath a curious telephone voice when feeling formal or trying to impress, which was most of the time. Sometimes, if there was a lull in the conversation, he would take the opportunity to recite some of his poetry in the telephone voice. People would quickly find something to say.

'I often feel that the motorway is the modern river — "On tides of tarmac/we travel our trends."' (He self-quoted.)

Toby cut into the versifying, ''Ow does it look, Doc? Yer can tell us straight, like.'

'Now, what we have here,' Demetrius began, 'is essentially a conflict of interests, compounded by a multiplicity of needs . . . Nico needs to work in order to buy heroin, and heroin in order to work; Echo needs Nico to buy heroin in order not to work; we, on the other hand, have but one simple need: Adventure.'

He pulled a Vick inhaler from his waistcoat pocket and took a deep sniff.

'Aaaah . . . Yes, gentlemen, Adventure. After all, is that not why we are gathered here now? There are other rewards in life, to be sure, but they are brittle and transient. Adventure sustains the Spirit, feeds the Will, makes us rise above our miserable subjectivity . . . unlike friend Echo, who prefers to wallow in his. A victim of unquestioning dogma, Echo crucifies himself for imagined sins.' He poked a Trust House Forte biro at Toby. 'Are we to stand motionless at the foot of the cross, in some bizarre Pietà of indecision?'

'Don't ask me, squire, I jus' want me cab fare back ter Wythenshawe.'

'May I suggest, Toby, that you set your sights a little higher than the windswept council estates of south Manchester? A golden egg of opportunity has been placed in our fragile nest. Let us endeavour to incubate it with our support, so that it may hatch into full plumage.'

'I'm not sure I catch yer drift,' said Toby.

Demetrius sighed, scratched his beard, and shook a couple of Valium from a small brown bottle (his father owned a chain of chemists). 'Quite simply. Keep Echo off the stuff, and keep Nico on her feet . . . I'm relying on you both. I've already redirected the career aspirations of that degenerate little free-loader with the septic leg who lived on her floor. "Artistic Adviser" indeed. An unfortunate attachment – though I suppose abscess makes the heart grow fonder.' He chuckled to himself and necked the valium. 'It's up to us now to take care of her. Remember, this is "Nico", "Chanteuse of the Velvet Underground". Buy yourselves some dark sunglasses and a couple of black polonecks . . . we'll need the art crowd behind us if we intend to make a go of this.'

He handed us three £10 notes each. Toby immediately went out and bought half a gram of heroin.

The days zigzagged into an endlessly frustrating stop/start come/go nowhere affair. Cabs from Demetrius's office over to Echo's and back again. Mysterious journeys down dark country lanes in the Saddleworth Moors, looking for Nico's heroin connection; or through the windtunnels and concrete labyrinths of the Hulme and Moss Side estates where the ice-cream men sold amphetamine before smack became more profitable. Suffer little children.

Nico-Watching: scanning her features for vestiges of that flawless beauty that I'd only ever glimpsed in a dim bedroom hopelessness, tuning into a voice that had only ever accompanied the late-night confessional elegy for a lost virginity.

In photographs the light seemed to carve and recreate her, like living sculpture, slicing into those granite cheekbones, chiselling the profile. Close up it was a different picture. The long blonde hair of the Chelsea Girl was now a greying brown, her facial skin puffed and slack, her hands and arms scabbed and scarred by needletracks, and her eyes like a broken mirror. It wasn't necessarily the years that had been unkind to her – she was only forty-two – but the woman herself. She had simply traded in her previous glamorous image for something altogether more unappealing. Yet she didn't seem to care, insulated from self-appraisal by the warm, nullifying reassurance that heroin provides. She'd locked herself in so deep that she hadn't surveyed the exterior in a while.

I couldn't work out how to talk to her. She spoke her own language . . . dreamy, cryptic. It was pointless trying to engage her with anodyne topics like current events or even music. But then, I was beginning to learn that musicians don't talk much. It's not that they're enigmatic or interesting. They just have nothing to say.

I didn't know if she was particularly unhappy, just strangely absent. Occasionally she'd throw out a casual remark like, 'I haven't had a bath in a year, you know.' What was I supposed to say? From day one she remarked on a certain fastidiousness.

'You're like a girl,' she'd say, 'always preening.'

My academic preoccupations amused her as well.

'How's life in Ox-foord?' she kept on asking, knowing perfectly well that 'life' and 'Oxfoord' viewed each other with mutual distaste. 'Such a pretty town . . .' and then she'd laugh. 'Pretty' meaning exactly that to her: ornamental and useless. Girls were 'pretty' . . . and a nuisance; she made it clear they would not be a welcome addition to our company with their 'squeaky little voices' and 'teeedious love lives'. Then her mouth would take on a sneer and she'd lapse once more into silence, her thoughts pursuing themselves in a tumbling morphine rush . . .

'Ah, poor Nico,' said Demetrius. 'Down what dark and empty avenues must the nightingale fly?'

After a week of near-total inertia, broken only by the sporadic tuning of guitars, I began to realise that a future with Nico was in fact an invitation to the land where time stood still and where lost causes returned to inert promise. I knew the territory. It was just like a library.

Demetrius had pulled us all together from different corners of his life, expecting some sort of golden alchemical reaction. But we remained a bunch of base metal misfits, hitching up our rusty wagon to Nico's celebrity in the hope that it might take us somewhere, anywhere. As her 'manager' he tried to keep a grip on things, but his authority was undermined by his appearance. Fatter than a cream cheese bagel, undersize trilby perched precariously on his bald head, he lumbered around Echo's place, crushing the children's toys, tripping over lead-wires, Caliban in a Burton suit.

Even when we got down to some serious attempt at a rehearsal, it was hopeless. No one knew what to do. It didn't matter how clever or proficient you might be (in fact, in Rock terms these are negative qualities), you couldn't fake the stuff. Either you felt it or you didn't.

A group of musicians have to find some purpose that unites them, apart from money. Pop groups are only gangs of pre-adults huddling together, finding a mutual coherence or security in the same two-chord language. Once they start to become individuals, curious and critical, then the thing falls apart and they grow up. It's a way of prolonging adolescence. We were all grownups except for Toby, and Nico wasn't really a team player.

Nico had ideas in her head but she couldn't communicate them, at least not precisely enough to convince everyone. But she knew when it worked and when it didn't, and the frustration was starting to get to her.

'No. No. Don't play it like that,' she would say to me. 'Play it more repetitiously . . . the same thing over and over.'

She was right. But I couldn't do it. I'd always want to embellish. The secret was that every time you picked up an instrument it had to be like the first time. No amount of fancy gadgetry or effects could simulate directness and intensity. Trouble was I knew my scales.

Toby would 'Clack Clack Clack' the drumsticks, to lead us into a song, but the response would be ragged and indifferent, a splutter of notes, instead of one affirmative chord.

There was no way out except 'out'. So I stayed at the piano and played:

DEAD DEAD

over . . . and over . . . again.

'That's nice,' said Nico.

Echo and I joined Demetrius at the Isola Bar.

'Fame is an exacting science,' he remarked, over a full English breakfast, 'and the famous are continually being tested.' He held up a tomato-shaped ketchup dispenser. 'To arrive at a three-dimensional image of oneself that can be engraved upon the contemporary consciousness, one has to eradicate that bitter-sweet fourth dimension of doubt.' He squirted a bright red blob on to his fried eggs. 'Doubt equals Irony equals Collapse equals Failure . . . Pass the sugar.' Distractedly stirring his mug of tea, he continued, 'Fame, James, projects a gigantic shadow of loneliness upon the world. Yet to want to be alone is as impertinent a wish as it would be for most of us to desire instant celebrity.' He sipped from his mug with a delicately-crooked pinkie. 'Famous people do not have private lives and they are never alone . . .'

'. . . even when they're dyin' from an overdose,' added Echo.

Nico's life seemed to be refined down to interviews which, in turn, were further distillations of a constant dialogue she enacted with herself.

A man and a woman sit silently in the control room of a radio station. He's young, about twenty-five, fresh-faced, fair hair, pastel-framed glasses, baggy sweatshirt. She's of a certain age, long brown hair turning grey, dressed in a morning coat and a black leather wristband with silver skulls. There's a record on the turntable, 'Femme Fatale'; the song's about to end.

> . . . - - -'- / - - - - - / - -/ - - - - / - - - / - - - / - / - - - -
> - - - / - - -'- / - - - -
> '- - - / - - - - - - - - - - / - - - - -
> - - -'- / - / - - - - - / - - - - - - . . .

[Permission to reproduce lyrics refused]

D.J.: Heyyyy . . . We're Piccadilly Radio. It's eight forty-five and I have here with me in the studio the original Femme Fatale herself . . . the *Legendary Nico*, singer with the *cult sixties* group the *Velvet Underground* . . . Created by *pop-art* supremo himself Mr Andy Warhol . . . Welcome to Manchester, Nico.

NICO (*pause*): That song . . . It's not about me . . . I just sang it . . . a long time ago.

D.J.: Right. Right. OK, Nico, before we talk about what you're doing now and why you're in Manchester, can we retrace our steps a little, just for our listeners?

NICO: If we have to.

D.J.: You come from *Berlin* originally, I'm told?

NICO: (*groans*): Oh . . . (*sighs*) Yes . . . well . . . nearly . . . kind of . . . not exactly . . .

D.J.: Now, er, that city has a special *mystique* . . . the *Nazis* . . . '*Cabaret*' an' all that . . . What was it like?

NICO: I didn't like it. I thought it was all rather tasteless.

D.J.: Tasteless? That's a rather unusual way to describe it.

NICO: You know . . . Overdone. That Liza Minnelli, she can't keep her mouth shut.

D.J. (*confused*): Liza Minnelli? Oh yeah, yeah . . . No, I meant, when you were young, that special *mystique* of *Berlin*.

NICO: Young? Mystique?

D.J.: Well, you know, they say Berlin was a kind of happening, dangerous, *action* kindovaplace.

NICO: Oh, yes, plenty of danger . . . The buildings falling down around you . . . The streets full of dust, you choked . . .

D.J.: Dear oh dear, Nico, that sounds pretty awful. Anyway, you began modelling in the fifties?

NICO: We had to live in the country. At night you could see the city burning, the sky red as blood . . .

D.J. (*coughs. Tries to clear a way out*): The War, a terrible time on both sides —

NICO: . . . The smell of burning buildings on the wind.

D.J.: OK . . . This is Piccadilly Radio and I've just been talking to Nico of the fabulous *Velvet Underground*. (*Jazzy voices: 'Picc-adilly Ra-dio . . . Manchester's Numero U-ni-o.'*)

'Enough!' Dr Demetrius slammed off the car radio.

'What *does* she think she's doing?' He pounded a heavy, leather-gloved hand on the steering wheel. 'Makes me look like a total nebbish . . . Here I am, trying to stop her career going down the toilet, while she's just flushing away . . .' He yanked off his glasses and rubbed his eyes. The car swerved out of lane.

'Steady Doc,' said Toby, putting a hand on his shoulder.

Dr Demetrius was a man under siege. The creditors were closing in. The Philistines were at the gate, dropping brown paper envelopes through the letterbox.

'I must make a phone-call . . . I don't know why I'm doing it for her.'

'*I* know,' said Echo slyly.

'Oh really? What do *you* know?'

'I know that you're no kosher medicine man . . . "Doctor".'

'I see no reason to justify my existence to a creature whose inability to even get out of bed puts him little higher in the evolutionary chain than an invertebrate slug.'

'An' you'd be a man of backbone, eh? Demetrius Erectus . . . I've seen the polaroids. Enough ter stiffen the resolve are they?'

Demetrius lifted his trilby and wiped his pate with a stiff, grey handkerchief.

'Dear God, this is not the life for a searcher after Truth . . . for one who seeks a poetic reality. The days of the great impresarios are gone. What room is there in this squat, tawdry business for a man of substance and vision?'

Echo slipped something into my hand – a polaroid photograph. A picture of Demetrius in a girl's white frock, so tight on him you could see each bulge of fat. He was bending over a chair, his naked behind raised up in the air, red lipstick smudged across his lips, his head turned towards the camera. He had a dark, possessed look in his eyes and a weird, almost disembodied grin. I handed it back to Echo. He leaned over and whispered in my ear.

'I've got a cupboardful on 'im . . .'

Demetrius caught us in the rear-view mirror.

'The Whisperers, forever relegated to the back seat of life, yet always ready to butt in with their miniature version of reality . . . Why don't you damn well learn to speak up, Echo?'

He whammed on a Tammy Wynette tape.

It was raining. Manchester was golden. At night, when the yellow streetlights reflect from the wet pavements and the cathedrals of the cotton barons glower sternly in the dark, you would not be mistaken in thinking it the most beautiful city in England.

'*There*'s a phone,' said Demetrius.

He double-parked beside it and got out.

The telephone was Dr Demetrius's umbilical link with a more stable world. Long before the mobile phone became such an essential accessory to urban dementia, Demetrius was trying to make the connection. It was territorial. Like a dog pissing on a lamp-post.

He banged on the window. Toby leaned over and wound it down.

'Anyone got a 10p?'

No one had a 10p. He scuttled off to the all-night chemist on the corner.

Hair lacquer was hanging thick in the air, the smell of cheap perfume, aphrodisia to all but the mean-hearted. They were crowding into Fagin's, the fantasy palace of the Wicked Lady and the Snowball, where the drinks were as sweet as the perfume, but less alcoholic. Echo and I looked at the girls. That's where we wanted to be, leaning against the wall, standing in the shadows of love, watching them dance around their handbags. The sexiest sight in the world.

Demetrius came back with a paper bag full of disposable syringes. ('It's a beautiful thing, but I can't use it,' said Nico the day before, handing him back a giant stainless-steel surgical hypodermic.) It was an instant 'open-sesame' having the title Doctor on his cheque book, people were always ready to ingratiate themselves.

'I'm tired out.' He sagged, breathless, into the driver's seat and started up the engine.

Echo and I blew kisses to the angels in the rain. They were yelling rendezvous to each other across the street, stamping their white stilettos impatiently, bare white legs blue veined with cold.

'They're not bothered about the weather,' said Echo, 'they're used to it. Everyone knows it's always rainin' in Manchester.' He curled up in the corner of the seat and wrapped himself in a dirty old blanket Nico used to protect her harmonium.

We turned into Piccadilly.

'Bloody night,' said Demetrius. 'Windscreen wipers on the blink again . . . Toby, get in the back with Jim and Echo. And give the screen a wipe while you're out there, would you?'

Toby grabbed the cloth perfunctorily. ''Ow come it's always yours truly that gets the soggy end of the rag?'

'Because you're a drummer,' said Demetrius. 'Drummers are another primitive life-form, of little use except as beasts of burden.'

She looked sad and incongruous, standing there in the rain.

'Why didn't you wait in the reception?' asked Demetrius.

'I just wanted to get out of that place. That guy was an aaasshole.' She threw a half-smoked Marlboro into the gutter and immediately lit another.

'I mean, why do they even *pretend* to be interested? . . . We could talk about something else . . . Always the same old shit . . . Berlin . . . The Velvet Underground . . . Who fucking cares? I don't.'

Demetrius hummed along to the cassette.

'Please turn that shit off.' Nico blew her cigarette smoke in his face. Demetrius coughed and switched off the cassette.

'Always the Velvet Underground . . . I want to talk about *my* records.'

'No one buys your records,' said Demetrius.

'That's because no one plays them!'

'Not many people are that depressed.'

'You've got some nerve, fixing me an interview with a moron like that . . . Do you know the kind of music he plays? Disco.'

Demetrius went into a mock-Yiddish routine:

'She don't like da Disco music. She don't like da Country & Western. I fix her an interview vid a nice young Goy . . . She don't like da interview . . . Vat's da matta mit chew? . . . I tell her, da Radio 3 people, dey're busy, dey already booked an interview vid Beethoven . . . I say to dem "But he's deaf" . . . "So vot?" day say, "Nobody listens to good music no more anyway."'

'Cra-a-zy,' said Nico, shaking her head.

We swung into Sunnyview Crescent. Demetrius put his arm around her a little earnestly, like a lover might do, and saw her to the step. They exchanged a few words and, as he gave her a kiss goodnight, he slipped something into her hand. She smiled. Everything would be all right again.

On the way back into town, Dr Demetrius yawned. Every day a new plan and a new problem.

'Anyone else fancy driving for a bit?' The only other driver was Echo and he was nodding out on the back seat.

Demetrius clocked him in the rear-view mirror. 'Pathetic,' he confided in his booming undertone to Toby and myself. 'To see a grown man with responsibilities indulge himself like a child. We're all aware of Nico's arrested development. But one child's enough! Either he gets his fingers out of her crib or he gets himself back on the dole queue.'

We stopped at the lights on Princess Park Way.

'Will you just look at that?' Demetrius tutted in commiseration and pointed to a twisted, crippled figure standing by the kerb.

The figure began to jerk and twist himself across the road, twitching and grimacing. His chin was tucked to one side and his right arm kept making a peculiar, arc-like, bowing motion.

'What right have we to self-pity . . .' asked Demetrius as the cripple dragged himself past our car, '. . . when there are poor suffering bastards like that in our very midst, wandering and lost?'

'Yeh,' said Echo, opening his one good eye to review the pitiful tableau, '. . . an' *I've* got 'is violin.'

CHILDREN OF THE POPPY

Echo had an itch. He scratched his arm until the skin was red and raw and his crown of thorns tattoo seemed to weep blood.

We were outside his place, blocking the pavement with old black flight-cases.

'So Jim – Jimmy – James . . . 'ow come yer packin yer axe, as they say, in this neck o' the woods? I wouldn't have thought Rock 'n' Roll was exactly your button, old bean.'

'Job,' I said. 'I need a job.'

'I thought they decided on 'oo wuz the Sons of Learnin' an' 'oo wuz the Children of Toil first day of infants school.'

'Then we're doomed,' I said.

He sniffed, his raw amphetamine-eroded nostrils flaring slightly. 'Can't see the attraction for yer.' He nodded at the clapped-out van and the flight-cases with the fading names of long-defunct groups stencilled in grey on the side.

A major pop group might employ a fleet of fierce articulated trucks loaded with lighting, sound equipment, stage sets, wardrobe, merchandising, even a few instruments – indeed the whole panoply of hardware that goes with the raw vitality of the people's music. Ours was a small affair. The glamour went no further than Nico.

Quite how Demetrius had managed to persuade her that it was necessary she perform with a group, I couldn't work out. But none of us would have been going anywhere if it were not for his persistence and her gullibility. Without us she would be able to travel in comfort and earn more money. It didn't make sense.

'She's not so thick as yer think, Jim – Jimmy. Don't forget, she's got the songs – what've you got?'

Perhaps Nico knew she was better when she sang alone. Maybe she wanted the spotlight to ease up on her for a while. Who could tell? She seemed so knowing and so credulous at the same time that it permanently wrong-footed you. You never knew where she was or where you stood in relation to her. Most of the time she disdained even to speak so there was no point trying to figure it out. We were here, that was all. The job was to load up this Mister Whippy van with Echo's broken-down junk and pretend to be something.

Demetrius must have got the truck from someone who owed him one. The seats were the kind of thing you get on public transport, the bare minimum in terms of comfort. Plastic and metal. No head-rests. We had to travel two thousand miles there and back in this. Nico hadn't seen it yet; I just knew she was going to tear into Demetrius when she clapped eyes on it. The MIND THAT CHILD warning was still visible beneath the thin coat of pale blue paint. On the side was written, in lean-to letters to suggest velocity, 'R & O VAN HIRE SALFORD'. The suspension sank with an ominous jolt each time we threw a case in the back.

After five minutes we stopped for another fag.

'But yer must 'ave some ulterior motive for climbin' aboard The Good Ship Nico? Lemmesee . . . it's not the Rock 'n' Roll cos yer know too many chords, an' it can't be the drugs cos yer've always got yer train fare 'ome . . .'

'It must be the sex then.'

'Good grief . . . yer can't be serious. Sex? This is a *junkie* group. Yer do this when yer can't do anythin' else.'

'Then we're both free to pursue our separate interests,' I concluded.

Toby struggled up the path putting all his weight behind the massive flight-case that housed his drum kit. Echo and I watched him anxiously.

'Don't just fookin' stare . . . give us a bit of shoulder.'

We shoved the reluctant crate up Echo's garden path, the

silly little castors getting stuck in every dip and hollow. Finally we reached the back of the truck. We needed a ramp. The thing was impossible to lift. We needed proper men.

Demetrius appeared. 'The shape of the legs is unimportant – but a finely turned ankle, that's the thing, *n'est-ce pas*, gentlemen?' He was towing an overstuffed leatherette suitcase on runners with a stick attachment – the kind of thing old ladies have. Under his right arm he carried a Bullworker. He dropped the Bullworker onto Toby's flight-case and parked his suitcase alongside.

'It's somehow deeply satisfying to see the working classes lathering up a good sweat. Like shire horses. I exempt you of course from this, James, though for some unaccountable reason you wish to align yourself with the lower orders.' He sniffed his Vick inhaler. 'Breasts and buttocks for *them*, eh?' He nodded at Toby and Echo. 'But the ankle, the asterisk, the footnote to the sonnet that is woman . . .'

'Get that fookin' bag of shag-mags an' dirty drawers away from my gear . . . Now!' Echo snapped.

'You want to know why you people will never be anything?' said Demetrius, snatching his bag. 'Can't take a joke.'

'Want ter know why yer'll always 'ave dirty underwear?' said Echo, ''Cos yer shit yerself when someone looks yer in the eye.'

The stand-off was broken only when Mercy, Echo's youngest, came up to us. She was about seven. Beautiful. Skin a soft golden colour. She was carrying a bunch of lily-of-the-valley, which she gave to Toby.

'Thank you, my little dear.' Toby bent down and kissed her on the forehead.

There was something other-worldly about the child, but anyone who spent their days playing among gravestones would be that way. She had power. The little girl could even subdue Demetrius, and he was an angry mountain in whose shadows the natives trembled. Or so he liked to think.

After we'd finished Toby, Echo and myself stared at the van, loaded to the gunwhales with crap. Demetrius was indoors being fed by Echo's wife.

'The suspension's gone – before *Faticus Omnivorus* has even sat in it,' Echo sneered.

We crawled across town, Demetrius at the wheel. We had to pick up Nico and Raincoat the sound engineer. Echo kept his head down and his hat over his face, so none of his friends would recognise him.

The van chugged into Sunnyview Crescent. Echo grabbed Toby's lily-of-the-valley and hopped out. 'I'll get her.'

'Creep!' said Demetrius.

We waited.

'Purra tape on,' said Toby.

Demetrius rattled through the pile in the glove-compartment. None of them had names or titles. How was anyone supposed to know? He chose one of his own: A Golden Hour of Conway Twitty.

I began to feel nervous. Strangely, it had never really hit me before that we were illegal. I started to make a mental list of the possibilities: possession of controlled substances; dubious credit cards; unsafe vehicle; illegally parked; loitering. Not forgetting crimes against good taste.

They came out, Good Queen Bess and Raleigh. Echo was staggering in front, carrying the harmonium like a relic of state. Nico had on a pair of aviator shades. It wasn't sunny and she wasn't smiling. She reached the gate and stared expressionlessly at the van, then looked back at Echo and shook her head.

Echo staggered, shell-shocked, in no-man's-land, still cradling the harmonium. He looked at her and he looked at the van, then turned and followed Nico back to the house. The door slammed shut.

Demetrius wasn't ready for this. It was the first time he'd been out of the country since he was a kid. This was his chance to break the grip of a fear that had been holding him in for years. It wasn't Nico. It wasn't us. It certainly wasn't the music. For him it really was an adventure. An adventure of the heart. Like falling in love, it contained the same terror and exhilaration. No one was going to spoil his romance.

His fist pounded the dashboard. He looked over at the

silent, shuttered house. 'That malignant little earworm, he's eaten into her soft mind already.'

He jumped out of the van, held on to his trilby, staggered a little at the hard shock of the ground, then straightened himself up for action. Manager/Parent/Suitor – this would test all three.

Echo drove us back to Demetrius's office. This time we walked up as there was no 'Dr' Demetrius to command respect. Tommy the Lift just spat on the floor and swigged at the bottle of Jameson's he kept under his stool.

The office was strangely full of activity. There was a guy on one phone talking to his record company. In the other room were two small women. One was pretty beneath the attitude armour. The other was pure testosterone. She might have made a good pitprop. They were both using the other phone, fixing up a show where they came in dressed entirely in animal entrails. It was some kind of statement. It was hard to find a good tune anywhere.

Cardboard boxes were stacked high. I looked inside one. It was full of unpromoted promo-singles for Pete Shelley's "Tiller Boys".

'Why does he keep all this stuff?' I asked.

The pretty one shrugged. The pitprop said, '*We're* here to make essential calls. What are *you* here for?'

'I honestly don't know . . . I thought I was doing a tour of Italy with Nico. But I haven't got further than Didsbury.'

'Oh, you've joined the good Doctor's sick list have you?' The pretty one smirked to the other: 'They all follow the Big Quack around, like ducks in a line.'

'Quack,' said pretty.

'Quack. Quack,' said pitprop.

Toby and Echo looked at me from the other room, puzzled.

It was clear this was no longer Demetrius's office. Who *were* these people? I pulled Echo to one side.

'Who *are* they?' I asked.

'People with careers,' he said.

Flying was the only way to be in Italy on time. It had made the most sense all along, but Demetrius was in favour of *terra firma*.

Raincoat

His eyes blinked, like a lizard. He had a smile like a lizard, totally insincere . . . maybe he would eat you. He would be smiling at you, summing up your calorific value as you chatted to him, a juicy buzzing fly. He always agreed with you so you never knew what he was really thinking.

Demetrius wanted all his friends involved. Jobs for the boys. All the way down the line. And the line stretched round the block to where someone's wallet was unaccountably £10 lighter, or someone else needed a runner for a couple of grams. That was where you'd find Raincoat.

But he was so charming. Truly charming. He'd been a ladies' hairdresser after he left school. He knew what women wanted. He shared their confidences and he got to know their tricks of the trade. He was a professional flirt. He could make a woman feel really good, adored.

In this way he would attach himself to strong professional women who might be feeling insecure about their femininity after a hard day breaking balls in the boardroom. He kept house for a smart young Irishwoman who ran a theatre company. She knew what he was really about but there was a kind of unspoken truce between them so long as he hoovered the house, fixed the dinner, called the plumber and performed prolonged oral sex on her every Friday night. This he was happy to do. It was a small inconvenience for a rent-free existence.

I recognised him before we were introduced. His name had flitted like a ghost through conversations. Nico was continually asking after him, probably because he knew exactly where to find what she was always looking for. Toby had known him for years. Echo, though, was uneasy about him . . . he'd lent him a microphone a few months back. Raincoat had promised to return it but Echo knew it had been traded in for dope. Echo kept a strict inventory of the junk in his cupboard. 'Whenever I look at 'im, I don't jus' see a second'and Sinatra, I see the microphone on a stand.'

Raincoat was standing by the check-in desk at Ringway Airport. 'We'll get high, starry eyed.' Like Demetrius, he was fond of a trilby but this one fitted, and had a beautiful red feather in the band. He had on a brown Donegal tweed suit with a yellow-checkered waistcoat and had his raincoat slung over one shoulder. He looked like an Irish bookie with Mafia aspirations. He looked good. But he'd left his soul a little too long under the dryer back at Vidal Sassoon's.

Raincoat, Toby and Echo were off the plane like a shot the minute the rear cabin opened. They mingled with the holiday-makers. Nico brushed past me as if I was a complete stranger, leaving behind her a wake of duty-free scent to baffle the 'sneefer' dogs. As I grabbed my hand luggage from the over-head locker a steward from Club Class tapped me. Would I follow him? 'Snow' clung to his uniform.

Club Class had been transformed into the Christmas Experience. 'Snow' everywhere . . . small fragments of white styrofoam that had burst free from a pillow Demetrius had chewed and then ripped apart as the aircraft tear-dropped over Milan airport. He cowered in the corner of the cabin like a trapped beast. The last pair of Euro-execs were disembarking: '*Drogisti*,' said one to the other, brushing the snow off his Armani lapels.

Demetrius was babbling a psycho peptalk: 'It's a matter of centring . . . Locating the Axial Body Meridian . . . tapping into the Kundalini . . .'

He breathed in deeply, yogically, on his Vick. Somewhere in the middle of Dr Demetrius was a thin hippy desperately signal-ling to be let out.

The promoters stepped through the automatic sliding doors. A girl and two guys. The men looked tough, but it was only fashion-tough. Beneath the stubble quivered career anxiety, inside the leather pants was soft pasta flab. Their eyes scanned the arrival lounge. They seemed to look through us, past us, around us, but never directly at us.

Nico stood there, slightly apart, an extra on life's battle-field, in her black rags. You could read them. After they'd eliminated all the other possibilities, could *this* be her? The Bag-Lady of Rock'n'Roll.

'Neeeeee-co!' The girl strode forward, grinning manically. 'Here, in Italia, at last.'

'Are we late?' Maybe Nico was joking. Behind the shades nobody knew. She wanted to go directly to the hotel. The promoter wanted to take her to a press meeting.

Nico had other plans. Other needs. 'I need to freshen up.' She stomped off to the hotel in her motorbike boots, the straps of which she never bothered to buckle. With Nico, you always heard her spurs first.

The promoters quickly consulted each other. The girl ran after Nico.

The guys introduced themselves. 'Benedetto.' 'Pasquale . . . and that is Titz, as everyone call her.'

Echo MC'd for us.

'Is there no one more?' Pasquale asked.

'He's following on a bit later,' said Echo.

I whispered to Raincoat, 'Don't you think we should wait?' He pretended not to hear.

'We also need ter "freshen up",' suggested Echo.

'Nico . . . she's blonde, no?' asked Pasquale as we sat in Milan's thrombosis of traffic.

'Nah,' said Echo, 'yer thinkin' of the Beach Boys.'

'In the photos, she's blonde,' insisted Pasquale.

'What photos?' asked Echo.

'In the Factory weeeth Andee Waaarhol and Velvette Onnergroun'.'

'Now I'm with yer . . . yer thinkin' of *Nico* from the *Velvet* Underground. Bit of a mix-up . . . we've brought yer *Narco* from the *London* Underground.'

Raincoat tried to friendly things up in a weird Esperanto all his own. 'Ah, La Bella Italia . . . Cappuccino . . . *La Dolce Vita* . . .' He racked his brain.

Benedetto picked up on the latter. 'Eh, *La Dolce Vita* . . . *Federico Fellini . . . Nico participo in quel film.*'

'Nico – yeh,' continued Raincoat, keeping up the cunni-lingua. 'Nico populario in Italia?'

'Boh!' Benedetto shrugged.

'*Pensavo che fosse bionda*,' said Pasquale to his pal, still preoccupied with Nico's hair colour.

'*Anch'io*,' said Benedetto.

Back at the hotel, the boys ripped open the pick-up plate on Echo's guitar and carved out the smack.

I fled to my room and laid out my pyjamas.

Demetrius installed himself in the Bridal Suite. Nico was aghast: 'Does he think someone will ma-a-ary him? The way he was on the plane . . . like a looonatic.'

I was scared. How many times had I been on stage? I counted, on one hand . . . two Barmitzvahs and a free-jazz jerk in Leeds. Nico was due to play a club in the north of Milan called Odyssea. Echo explained that the further out of town the venue, the uglier it is. I never went to clubs. Too loud. Too many people. A sea of piss in the gents. Echo and Toby reassured me that this was normal – people who played music rarely went to hear the stuff.

Then there were the songs. I still couldn't remember how they went and we only had to do seven. Toby said he'd nod to me every time I had to change chords. 'That'll impress the music critic of the Milan Bugle,' said Echo.

The tour bus tumbril picked us up at the hotel. Pasquale was at the wheel. The show was seven hours away but already I felt the game was up.

'Don't worry,' said Echo. 'You don't count, they're only interested in Nico, they want ter touch Death in drag.'

Demetrius sat in the front passenger seat. He loved the big screen. He had to devour everything. He'd showered himself in bonhomie and the hotel's complimentary aftershave.

'Jesus, you smell like a hooker's haaandbag!' shouted Nico, pinching her nose.

Pasquale jerked the bus to a stop.

'I say, steady on there, driver!' shouted Raincoat, unloading the last squirt of a shot into his naked buttock.

Pasquale helped me carry my keyboard into the club:

'Nico, ees a boy's name, no?'

'Yes, I think she'd like to be one . . . the boots, the bad manners . . .'

Raincoat, carrying Nico's shoulder bag, interrupted. 'Not fergettin' those teensy weensy temper tantrums . . . Like a geezer? No chance. No matter 'ow 'ard she tries, she'll never be able ter sing like Barry White or piss 'er initials in the snow.' He rummaged in her bag for any stray crumbs of dope or money.

Pasquale introduced Raincoat to the sound and lighting crew. They showed him the mixing desk: twenty-four channels, each with different EQs, a stack of effects – reverb, delays, a hundred different ways of taking a sound and placing it anywhere.

Raincoat shook his head: 'Nah, can't work with that lot, mate – pots 'n' pans, no good ter me. I've only ever used Trojan mixers . . . mucho regretto.'

The Italians were mortified. This equipment was the best in Milan. What was this Trojan stuff? 'Trojan?' 'Trojan?' They kept passing the word around like a hot pizza.

Demetrius loomed up. 'Does there seem to be a problem, gentlemen?'

''Ee say 'ee only work weeth Trojan equeepment,' complained the Italians in an Anvil Chorus.

'Trojan?' queried Demetrius. 'Do I know them? Are they by any chance related to Stag and Featherlite?'

'Eh?' Raincoat blanked him. 'No . . . yer know . . . Tro-jan. Built by Trond Jansson, Swedish . . . They're the tip-top of the tree, beautiful Scandinavian teak finish. This stuff's pots 'n' pans.'

A sudden rage shadowed Demetrius's face.

'My dear Raincoat, although the minutiae of public address systems are a matter of deep indifference to me, I am however aware that they operate on universal principles . . . Must I therefore construe that you are, in fact, an impostor?'

Raincoat shuffled from one foot to another. 'It's only pop,' he said.

Demetrius's eyes blackened over. Nero in a Lone Ranger mask.

'Listen, mate.' Raincoat's voice was dry, and insinuating. He smiled, a lizard on a hot rock. '*Listen*, she's the singer an' she can't sing; they're' – he pointed at me – 'the musicians an' they can't play; you're the road manager an' yer can't travel; I'm the sound engineer an' I can't fix me girlfriend's 'i-fi . . . What's the bleedin' diff'rence?'

5.00 p.m.: Echo was trying to assemble Nico's harmonium. Raincoat was twiddling randomly with the knobs on the mixing desk. Toby practised relentless paradiddles on a bar stool. Demetrius had gone to the bordello across the road to calm his nerves.

The dressing-room measured about thirteen foot by seven. A minimalist paradise. Wall-to-wall white tiles, buzzing strip-light, smoked glass and chrome coffee-table, black wire-mesh foldout chairs facing a wall-length mirror . . . cosy.

Nico sat there alone, her eyes closed, head resting back against the wall. A splash of blood laced across the white enamel sink, her signature.

Softly I closed the door and went to buy a postcard. Wish you were here.

8.00 p.m.: 'Sorry, can't eat.' My stomach was a twist of gristle. Demetrius took my plate and scooped the contents on to his own.

'Waste is a symbol of decadence,' he said.

'So is being faaat,' said Nico. 'Eat. Eat. Eat. What else do you do with my money?'

'I go a-whorin', ma'am, as befits the custom of an English gentleman.'

'Toooorist!' said Nico.

*

10.00 p.m.: There were fifteen, maybe more, in the dressing-room. Pasquale, Titz, some bespectacled dwarf with a dicta-phone recording everything Nico said, a couple of Versaces and an Armani with cameras and clinging girlfriends, an acne-ridden psycho babbling nonsense in Nico's other ear, and three people nobody knew at all, sitting on our chairs.

The dwarf asked each of us in turn our musical pedigree. Nico's of course was the hippest, then Echo and Toby. Eventually he got to me.

'An' wheech grups have you played een?'

'I . . . well . . . er . . .'

'Jim plays in a Palm Court orchestra,' butted in Echo.

'Napalm Court Orchestra? Eees Trash Metal?'

'Pure scrapyard,' I answered. He seemed gratified.

10.30 p.m.: Demetrius kicked them all out. Then Nico kicked him out. She didn't like the way he ogled her when she was taking a shot. 'Like I was naaaked.'

We were running late but she had to have one last hit before we went on stage.

I chain-lit another cigarette.

'Jim, look, yer makin' *me* nervous, an' I'm not in it,' said Raincoat. 'Go on, 'ave a dab, yer'll be all right.'

He opened a small white envelope and then from his waist-coat pocket he produced a miniature penknife. It was the prettiest thing, slightly curved, dagger-shaped. The body was ebony, with three diamonds set along the length. He pressed the middle diamond; a tiny blade flicked out, like a baby with a vicious tongue. He trimmed a corner off the pinkish brown powder and scooped it on to the blade. He held it under my nostril.

I heaved into the sink.

'Shiiit, Raincoat. Such a waste.' Nico tutted self-righteously, like a kindergarten ma'am. 'Don't you know he's a health freeek . . . probably a nymphomaniaaac too.' Moral superiority builds its pulpit in the strangest places.

10.45 p.m.: Perhaps it was the white tiles and the mirrors.

'I need a piss,' said Nico. Though it resembled one, there was no WC in the dressing-room and no other way out except through the audience.

Titz was thumping on the door. 'Can you pleeese be on stage *now?*' The audience were slow-handclapping. Nico hoisted herself on to the sink. We all looked the other way.

Pissssssssss . . . You could hear it in the pure tiled acoustics. We started giggling. So did Nico.

Titz banged on the door again. 'Tell that girl to shutthe-fuckup,' said Nico. 'How can I do it when she's making me *nerv*ous?'

Echo opened the door, blocking Titz's view. Her head peered round to witness a Rhinemaiden perched on the sink with ancient grey cotton drawers flapping down around her motorbike boots. Another illusion shattered.

Titz led us on stage with a flashlight. Echo first, then Toby, then me. Nico was still hitching up her pants.

Echo plugged into his amplifier, slung on his guitar strap, searched in his pocket for a plectrum, then very carefully and very intently he began to play. Maybe it was good, but no one out front could hear anything. He looked over at me. One word registered across his features. Raincoat.

Nico strode on. The audience immediately surged forward. She stood straight, head back, eyes closed, hand resting on the mike-stand, waiting.

Silence. Nico looked round at us inquiringly. Echo shrugged. Over at the desk I could see Demetrius and the Italians gesticulating at Raincoat. The sea of faces was looking mean. They'd paid good money.

Nico pointed upwards, as if to suggest more volume. As she did so a brain-searing whine shot through the place like a hot needle between the ears.

Toby counted 3–4 with his sticks and we started to play, a whizz-bang cacophony. But the more hideous the uncontrollable squawks and screams of feedback became, the more the audience were getting off on it. My electric organ sounded like a buzz-saw. Toby kept ripping into his snare, Echo was laughing and shaking his head in disbelief. Nico was pacing up and down the stage with her fingers in her ears, kicking at the nearest heads in the audience.

Back at the mixing desk, I could see Raincoat smiling, a huge beam of self-congratulation across his face . . . After all, it was only Pop.

The seven songs were soon over. Nico had dispensed with our services for the time being.

'What? You play no more?' asked Pasquale.

'Don't know any more,' said Echo.

'Wha'appen now?'

'The funeral begins.'

Disappointing to be back in the dressing-room after only twenty-five minutes. For Echo, though, a relief. He hated any kind of public display of anything. Toby, being the youngest, still had plenty of adrenalin to work off. He rat-a-tat-tatted his drumsticks on the tiled walls.

'Gizabreak, and abbreviate the Boys' Brigade, willyer?' said Echo, lighting the last of his No. 6. Toby stopped, mooched, and hunted for the beer crate. Plenty of Pepsi and Orangina and a weird Italian Tizer. (Demetrius liked to drink soda-pop. He'd drawn up the contract. Pop it would be. Twenty-four bottles. At every gig.)

'Maybe there's some action up front,' said Toby. 'Fancy takin' a look?'

We went sidestage and walked round the back of the audience. (Pop groups are the only practicable alternative for males who are too narcissistic to make the first move.) But instead of a host of Botticelli angels in miniskirts, Demetrius was waiting for us. Imperator. Surveying the scene of battle: 'There was a time, not so long ago, when people knew of no world other than their own.' Dr Demetrius was in reflective mood. 'They were better off for it. Life-connected to the seasons and the stars . . . Now their heads are full of rubbish, inane fifth-form poetry masquerading as art. They should be listening to Verdi and Puccini . . .' He pressed one nostril and Vicked the other. 'Er, need I mention that you were crap?'

'What d'yer expect, with a bookie's runner at the controls?' said Echo.

'Why not do something constructive then and fix up a proper sound for Nico's solo spot?'

Raincoat was still filling the room with weird electric jungle noises. Echo brushed him aside, slid a few knobs up and down, pressed a few settings, the basic stuff. Enough to place her voice somewhere.

We stepped back from the pain threshold. The ringing feedback stopped. The stage was now in total darkness except for a single spot from above. The audience seemed physically to ease up. A different feeling took over. Less mean, more intimate. It was a backstreet Punkerama, but people were willing it into a cathedral. They'd come to be part of some rite. It wasn't directly to do with the music, or even Nico, they just wanted to be somewhere else. So they were prepared to take her seriously, and she, in turn, was trying her best to take them seriously. A temporary deal had been struck with futility. She was pushing open, with their help, however slightly, the heavy oak doors upon the Mystery.

She sat at the harmonium. The instrument was nothing like a church harmonium — much smaller, about the size of a baby's coffin. To create a sound, she had to work the small bellows by way of pedals at her feet. With her right hand she played a repeated single phrase and with her left a melody. She'd carefully created her own harmonies, though she had no idea what the notes were in orthodox musical language.

And then of course, there was the voice. Dungeon-deep, where the secret horrors were hidden. It made you listen. No small achievement these days. Sometimes the words were nonsense, her own made-up juxtaposition of rhymes or words that just sounded intriguing coupled together. 'Nemesis on loaded wheels.' It made you wonder who was at the flight deck. It certainly wasn't the voice of a sixties chick in op-art pants, or some emotionally neutral piece of Manhattan window-dressing as had been envisaged by the Factory Funsters.

'This is the voice of one of those neolithic Venuses with the enormous pelvic girdles, and tiny mammalian heads that they dig up from the peat bogs of northern Denmark,' opined Demetrius.

Demetrius's mouth hung open. His glasses were filled with the beatific blue light that emanated from the stage.

> Unwed virgins in the land
> Tied up on the sand.

Something stirred inside Demetrius's overcoat.

> Are you not on the secret side?

Nico muttered off-mike into the wings. Pasquale appeared with a drink and placed it precariously on a corner of the harmonium. She shook her head and put it securely on the floor by her foot pedals. She started up the harmonium again. Maybe for her it was just that bit more interesting than a pedalo, but we were seeing it for the first time. It was a crazy act. A forty-two-year-old Valkyrie, spaced out in motorbike boots.

She stopped pedalling for a second, reached down for her drink and took a long, throat-saving swig. Instantly she spat out the sickly sweet guck and half-puked an enormous arc that cascaded through the spotlight beam.

FFFUUUCCCKKKK

It echoed on and on through the sound system from one speaker to another. Laughter in the cathedral.

'I'm going to fire you aaaall . . . Assholes!' She was sitting in Demetrius's seat in the bus back to the hotel. 'You're a bunch of rejects.' She went round each one of us. 'Invalids . . . freeee-loaders . . . nymphomaniacs . . . morons . . . shysters . . . Don't bother turning up for the next show . . . I'll have you all thrown out!'

'So . . . this is the predicament . . .'

We were gathered around the four-poster bed in Dr Demetrius's Bridal Suite, minus the bride.

'She's out of stuff already, hence the tantrum . . . although I must say, I find it unlikely that even Nico with her legendary appetite for self-destruction could possibly have cleaned up four grams in two days. I feel she must have had a little chivalrous assistance on the way.' He sneered at Echo. 'As for the sackings, *I* determine who stays and who goes . . . however, I'm afraid there will have to be a certain stringency regarding your immediate remuneration. I can't get another lira out of the Eyeties until we've done a few more shows. There's no recourse but to use what little cash we have in order to keep Nico pointing upwards –'

''Old on a minute,' interrupted Echo, ''oo's payin' fer *this* gaff?' He scanned the Bridal Suite.

Demetrius propped himself up on a pink satin cushion. 'I have certain personal, *private* funds at my disposal, but these are exclusively for my own use in an Absolute Emergency. This does not constitute an emergency, but rather a tiresome interruption in our joyous progress towards the golden South . . . much in the manner of Keats and Shelley, wouldn't you say, Echo?'

'What about the beers?' asked Toby.

' "With beaded bubbles winking at the brim",' continued Demetrius abstractedly. 'Perhaps something could be arranged with regard to the refreshments, we shall have to see . . . In the meantime, frugality, my friends, frugality.' He pulled a tasselled rope and the heavy velvet drapes fell round the four-poster bed.

I had regular sleeping habits, as did Nico, who preferred to sleep all day, fearing disintegration in daylight. I wanted to sleep but couldn't. Italy was out there – the bars, the bamboozle, the eternal city of flirts, but I felt distanced and disorientated . . . and tired.

In truth Italy was as far away as it had been back in Echo's parlour. What we were up to wasn't work exactly, but it wasn't a holiday either. As Echo said, it was what you did when you couldn't do anything else.

I couldn't seem to connect on any level with Nico. I was used to people who talked. Too much chat seemed to irritate her, too much silence made me nervous. I asked her if she wanted to go and see some frescoes. 'I can see them in a book.' A stroll maybe? Too far, too tired – the shows exhausted her.

People would give her things. Once, as we were leaving the hotel, a strange girl, emaciated and stricken, pressed a shell into her hand. Nico immediately passed it on to Echo who made the sign of the cross and threw it away. The girl, in Nico's eyes a witch, had been waiting up all night since the show, hanging around the entrance, hoping for a glimpse. 'Anyone who wants to see me that bad has got to be nuts.'

Nico seemed to keep going on a diet of chocolate and white wine. Demetrius would organise great feasts in an attempt at international conjugality. Nico would absent herself.

'I can't bear to think of all those lumps of food just *rotting* inside me.'

She said she hadn't had a shit in a couple of weeks. Echo said constipation was routine for a junkie. (Though he wasn't sure if, in his case, it was the smack as he could only go in his own 'po'.) I imagined Nico, once the gig was done, back at the hotel, curtains drawn, only the ghost flicker of TV, needle emptied, bathroom black, concentrated upon that still stubborn sphincter. Ole Dead Eye in the darkness, coldly staring at the stagnant latrine of romance, the Mediterranean.

Northern Europeans go to Italy to relax, to feel human again in a more exuberant and demonstrative culture, more loving and maternal than their own. North of the Alps it's the fight to stay warm. Nico had devised her own form of insulation – psychical and physical. (I noticed that even on cold days she'd often worn only a light shirt.) But when the smack ran out she soon got the shivers. It didn't matter in the least that we were beside the golden Mediterranean. Nothing outside really impinged on her terrifying single-mindedness, her obsessive neurological and emotional need for heroin. Even *La Dolce Vita* turned sour.

In Rome Nico got deep into withdrawal, her nerves scraping her bones. The money had shrunk, the shows were disappointing, the desperados were doing the drugs in very quickly. The promoters had arranged a lunch meeting with Italian *Vogue* for a possible photo session. Raincoat and Toby practised sucking in their cheeks. The pretty boys and girls dressed in their relaxed classics did not take immediately to Nico wrapped in an old blanket, eyes streaming, concerned only with her fee. I had an idea. Nico upholstered in Renaissance velvet, the needle scars on her tortured hands and arms, the grey flesh hanging lifelessly from those once unassailably high cheekbones. A powerful spread? There was some rapid consultation during which I heard the word '*pervertito*', then they shook our hands, wished us a successful tour and left. Within seconds I'd blown everyone's chance of a good lunch.

I felt especially ostracised after that until near the end of the tour in Genova, when I got my big break to go and get the drugs with Echo. (As I knew three Italian words, *Ciao*, *Vaffanculo* and *Arrivederci*, I had a use.) A smooth transaction with some charming Moroccans, marred only by the later discovery that they'd substituted the heroin with salt.

'A hundred bucks an' not even enough salt for a packet o' staffords,' lamented Echo.

Nico's reaction was less circumspect. 'Assholes.'

Things always ended up there.

A heavy black brogue inserted itself into my room – followed by a dark overcoat, beard, glasses, the soft pale skin of one who toileth not in the fields, hummingbird flash of Vick inhaler.

'James . . . I feel I must speak to you.'

I thought, This is it. My old pal Dr Demetrius come to administer the last rites.

'I wonder if you're altogether happy . . .' I'd heard it at the end of every job I'd ever had. '. . . with things as they are?'

'What can I do?' I asked. 'It's alien territory. The guys are

OK for a few seconds as they intersect normality in between getting out of their heads and sweating it out. The rest of the time it's lunacy . . . Nico hates me . . .'

'Perhaps you should ignore them – after all, they *are* little more than circus creatures. Their needs are very basic, their joys are commonplace.'

Things were stirring once more beneath the overcoat. From one of the voluminous pockets he pulled out a Bible. The page was marked with a membership card to 'Raffles. Gentlemen's Sauna Club.' The text was underlined.

> . . . thou knowest the people,
> that they are set upon mischief.
> For they said unto me
> 'Make us gods, which shall
> go before us . . .'
> (*Exodus* 32, v. 22–23)

'Unfortunately,' continued Demetrius, 'Nico comes from a long line of people without a God they can truly believe in and – worse still – without a sense of humour. She fails to see the entertainment value in a lugubrious piano player, a punk drummer and a dope-fiend guitarist. Nor, sadly – and this is particularly painful for me, James – does she reciprocate the depth of my affection for her . . . more than affection . . . *love*.'

So, it was '*amore*' after all. I was being employed to facilitate a romance.

In Genova we performed with an armed guard around the stage. Young Argentinians of Italian extraction were meeting their deaths in the South Atlantic. There was a strong anti-English feeling, especially among guys of conscription age.

The promoters had really pumped up Nico's reputation in their pre-concert publicity. The kids were expecting heavy metal Wagner – what they got was Demetrius's circus. Soldiers reconnoitring the stage; Nico wandering on and off, unsure of her lines, coming in with the right lyrics but to the wrong song. A strange ballet to cabaret angst.

'Beastly business, old boy,' said Demetrius in the dressing-room after the show. 'Do I take it you'll be yielding to the academic yoke once more next term?'

The study or the circus? The monastery or the madhouse? I looked around. Echo was helping Raincoat retrace his steps down memory lane to the exact moment when his microphone went missing. Nico was locked in her millionth interview about the Velvet Underground – why this, why that, why wasn't it still 1967? Toby was offering to show the rose tattoo on his backside to a couple of cat girls in leopardskin mittens – if they would, in turn, 'show somethin' of yer beautiful city ter me an' my pal'. He pointed me out. One of them darted a glance at me and giggled into her paws. She was pretty.

Nico stuck her head out of the interview and glared at me. 'Nymphomaniac!' she spat, and then carried on reliving Andy Warhol's dream. For all of us.

'See you next term,' I said.

CHEZ NICO

Schlaf Kindlein schlaf
Deine Mutter hüt die Schaf
Dein Vater ist in Pommerland
Pommerland ist abgebrannt
Schlaf Kindlein schlaf.

(Sleep, baby, sleep
Your mother guards the sheep
Your father's gone to Pommerland
Pommerland is burnt to the ground
Sleep, baby, sleep.)

Nico and Demetrius were crooning a hideous lullaby. Dr Lugubrious and Old Mother Hell in full-tilt fireside nostalgia. April in Paris, winter in Prestwich.

'My earliest memory is of Nanny Cristel singing to me.' Demetrius wiped his misty glasses. 'First she would dry my little pink body, wrap an enormous towel around me and then rub – ah, how she would rub . . .'

Echo poked the fire and spat. The gobbet of catarrh-green spume fizzing abruptly in the post-lullaby bliss.

Nico's bags were packed. It was the big send-off, though she was only moving one hundred yards round the corner. Faith didn't like other women in her kitchen, boiling up syringes all the time. And it shamed her to see Echo forever rolling up his sleeve in the hope of a free hit. Faith worried so much she couldn't eat; not that there was ever enough food to feed the whole tribe, including Nico and assorted ephemera. Why couldn't Echo be more of a man and look after his family, instead of being permanently incommunicado, brooding about his new mistress – heroin? It was like he was somewhere else all

'. . . Then she would shower me with baby talc, run the tips of her fingers down the warm yielding crack of my chubby behind and cradle my tiny testicles in her cupped hand . . . "There, my little man," she'd say, "there . . ." '

"There, my little man," she'd say, "there . . ." '

Knuckles on wood: Echo peeped through the kitchen curtains. Raincoat. He'd borrowed Demetrius's Citroën, ostensibly to take his lumbago-ridden grandmother to the physio, actually to make a run to his mate down the Moss.

'How's your poor grannie, Raincoat?' asked Demetrius, dropping his catch as Raincoat threw him the car-keys.

'Notser clever.' Raincoat slurred his words, his pupils like pinheads. 'But she sez t' tell yer that if there wuz more folk like good ol' Dr Demetrius, wha' a be'er world it'd be, feralluvus.'

Dead leaves still fluttered across the path as we carried Nico's things up to her new flat. It was the ground floor of one of those great Victorian Gothic villas built originally for Greek shipowners in the days when the Manchester Ship Canal was the main artery of commerce for King Cotton. Since the turn of the century they'd been a haven for Hasidic Jews fleeing the eternal pogrom of central Europe.

'Don't they look weeeerd?' said Nico, pointing to a huddle of bearded men and side-curled youths with prayer-white faces.

'I like the way they look,' I said, 'it's romantic.'

She examined them more closely, the eighteenth-century dress, frock-coats, gaiters, black hats. 'They don't wash, you know.'

'Neither do you,' I replied.

'I do . . .' she protested. 'I took a bath that time in Milan.'

Echo and Raincoat pulled up beside us. Demetrius remained in the car, listening to Country heartaches and feeding on some hot-potato latkes from the kosher kaff.

There was a figure, waving, at the bay window that over-looked the untended garden. Nico suddenly seemed overjoyed and rushed on ahead. Raincoat cast a glance up at the house. 'I see we 'ave Le Fils [pronounced Fills] with us, Le Vray Beau Jolly Newvo 'imself . . . Le Kid.'

'Her kid?' I'd forgotten about the son.

'Yeh,' said Echo, ' 'er very own creation. Yer gonna love 'im.'

'What's he called?' I asked.

'Ari.'

'Yeh.' Raincoat glowered up at the window. 'An' we're jus' wild about Ari.'

Ari, Le Kid, was about nineteen, the super-beautiful progeny of a union between the North and the Mediterranean, Nico and Alain Delon. Nico had a brief fling with Delon in her model days. Now Delon absolutely didn't want to know. Le Kid had turned up at the matinée idol's Paris apartment, only to be turned away by the maid. Even though Delon's mother took him in, Le Kid did not exist. Neither did he exist properly for Nico. While he was still in the womb she'd dropped acid along with the usual family favourites, and when he'd cried she found the most expedient solution was to lock him in a cupboard. It must have pained Ari to see pictures of that other Delon Jr, waterskiing with Princess Pixie of Monaco. Famous folk usually buy off responsibility with money – Nico hadn't got it, Delon wouldn't give it. Le Kid opened the door.

'*Maman. Maman.*' They embraced. He looked over her shoulder at us. His nose twitched in that Frenchified manner, like there was a bad *odeur*. Who were we? More shit she'd picked up on her boots. He turned away from us.

'*Maman . . . suis-moi, j'ai un petit cadeau pour toi.*'

We followed them down the hall, me walking backwards, clattering the harmonium against the walls.

'*Ferme les yeux,*' he said to her. I don't know why, but I did too. '*Bien . . . ouvre!*' He held out a shining new hypodermic, loaded and ready to go. Nico gasped with joy.

A truly loving son understands (and shares) his mother's needs.

The world had shrunk once again, to coal fires, TV game shows, tea drinking and cruel parlour games round at Echo's. Dr Demetrius's Great Adventure had shrivelled overnight. Nico was sitting tight. With a wallet-load of phony credit cards, and a pocket full of valium, Demetrius was happy to spoil her so long as she behaved herself. But the rest of us needed paid work. We'd do the odd one-off gig at Tiffany's, Bradford, just to take the instruments for a walk, but it was nothing like enough. Nico and Demetrius paid such a pittance, the only reward was glamour, and we certainly weren't getting any of that.

I did a one-night stint as a DJ at a regular Thursday 'Punk Night' Demetrius ran at Rotter's, a vomitorium cellar-club on the Oxford road. I played them one of Demetrius's records: K-Tel's *The Best of Roy Orbison*, 'as seen on TV'. 'Blue Bayou' all night long. It seemed a punk thing to do. Mohicans with spider-web cheeks and 'cut here' neck tattoos would come up: 'This is shite! Fuck off, cunt!' etc. They got really mad and started turning tables over, throwing bottles. I thought they'd had a good time, but Demetrius wouldn't let me do it again.

Then the rumour started. America. Everyone wanted to go, desperately, except for the star act and manager. Nico had really got to like the Iranian smack, she had a very strong reliable connection, she was getting stuff maybe fifty per cent pure – it would take a lot to prise her away from that.

'The Yank gear's dreck-powder,' said Echo. 'About five per cent kosher, not worth touchin' unless yer score about twenny grams an' yer've got works the size of a fookin' stirrup pump.'

Demetrius wanted to go, but couldn't. It would mean the neurasthenic's nightmare of being trapped in an aircraft again. 'Of course I'm not afraid,' he'd say, 'it's simply an infection of the middle ear that affects my balance. I believe astronauts can get it.'

Toby would often spend the cocktail hours in that great salon of *fin-de-siècle* languor Happy Times, a shooting gallery in Wythenshawe. Wythenshawe is one of those classic postwar answers to the perennial question: What Shall We Do With the

Working Class? If the poor must be forever with us, then at least let's keep them out of sight. It takes the best part of half an hour from Manchester city centre to get there.

'By the time the filth arrive, the entire contents of yer gaff 'ave bin nicked, resold, and some swine in Oldham's watching the Street on *your* telly,' said Toby. Toby lived at his mum's, a traditional Lancashire matriarch, who controlled with an iron grip a household of useless males. Three packs of cigs a day, crippling emphysema, but she'd still give them a good clout round the ear just for the sake of it.

At Happy Times you paid your fiver and you'd get a shot of smack or speed. Mr Happy Times himself just sat all the time in an armchair, monitoring everything from strategically placed mirrors, a .38 under a cushion on his lap. Purity of a kind.

America. You could get a good pair of shoes in America.

'There's all sorts of tackle in them Thrift Shops,' dreamed Echo. 'An' when we do L.A. we *must* stay at the Tropicana.' Echo couldn't overstress the importance of the Tropicana motel. Tom Waits lived there. Tom was the only man whose sartorial tastes Echo felt were as intriguing as his own. They shared a mutual passion – shoes. Echo had acquired six pairs on the Italian tour. He wondered if Tom also shared his misfortune in having small feet . . . it meant that certain coveted styles would never be in stock, and it made the hunt for the perfect pair that much more poignant. It was a theme whose constant tread reverberated throughout his daily life, possibly more urgent even than his routine search for mood-altering drugs.

America had everything. Flame-haired girls in cowboy boots who drank Bud from the bottle and told dirty jokes. Twisters, shapers, sharks and fraudies. People who could tell a good story . . . and they all lived at the Tropicana.

*

Back at H.Q. Echo, the pretext was rehearsal, but the reality was more sanguinary.

Nico hits the excited vein on the crown of her foot. Blunt needles, disappearing veins. A small trickle of blood weeps down the side. 'Even when you have the stuff, the needles are dead,' she says.

Echo was eyeing up the cottons that absorb any morphine sediment left in the spoon. (A bit like scraping up Mum's cakemix.)

'Auntie Nico?' It was little Mercy. 'Have you hurt your foot?'

'Not now, chuck.' Echo steered the child towards Faith in the kitchen.

Faith was scrubbing away the shame, furiously trying to maintain a semblance of domestic normality, as if this was a typical suburban household with a slightly eccentric aunt from Germany on an extended visit. She'd guard the children's lives from any accidental encounter with the arcane and perplexing objects that attended Nico's habit. Bent spoons held over sacred flames, sharp syringes – the shining vessels of faith, mysterious scars on her man's arms – the stigmata. For a Catholic girl it was a monstrous sacrilege, the hideous mirror of her family's degradation.

But we were all hooked on something. We'd all been connected by Demetrius's need for stimulation. He liked to experiment with personalities, test loyalties against each other. Like a bizarre *shadchen* or matchmaker, he was curious to see what issue would arise from such unlikely marriages of temperament. It became impossible to distinguish who was using whom, forms of desperation were so varied: Drugs, Money, Sensation, Sex, Travel, Change, Adventure. We'd claimed our appropriate share of these from him in exchange for the subjugation of our individual will. It would be too grandiose to call it a Faustian bargain, yet, on our own gossipy malodorous level, there was the slight stink of sulphur about it, a cloven hoof impressed upon the seal.

*

I was taking a piss in Echo's bathroom. Children's clothes, mould, never dry. I could hear Nico and Demetrius talking outside the back door.

'. . . always hanging around. Why? The more of them, the less for me. I can go to America aloone.'

'Most inadvisable, Heartette. Singermann' – the U.S. promoter – 'has specified a group. America wants Rock 'n' Roll. You'll be performing for audiences who revere the sacred memory of the King Himself. Much as I love you on your own with the harmonium – the singer/sewing machine – one has to think theatrically, Nico. I must urge you to see the professional sense in performing with a group.'

Nico was silent . . . there was a lot to assimilate. Then I heard her say, 'But them?'

'Darling one, what d'you expect? They come cheap.'

'Even so, they're always eating – and yooooo tooooo.'

Demetrius coughed. 'Errr – they use up a lot of energy.'

'Not on the music they don't . . . That Jim, with the girls all the time . . .'

I blushed. I was hearing my death sentence.

'He's classically trained.'

'He sure is . . . he won't play like *I* want. That stupid synthesiser thing he's got, he has no idea. He makes it sound like a kazooooo or something . . . reedeeculouss.'

'He's very good,' Demetrius insisted. 'He plays a charming little study by Erik Satie: "Gymnasium" or something . . . how does it go? Dum da di da, da di dum da di da . . . or is it da di dum, da di da da di dum?'

Silence again.

'And Echo.' (I was not to die alone.) 'I just wish he wouldn't bug me for stuff all the time.'

'I've arranged for him to see Dr Strang up at Prestwich . . . once he gets a methadone script he'll stop bothering you.'

'I don't know . . . there's the money . . .'

'*Your* fee is assured, my sweet. I'm sending my best lieutenant – Bags – along. He's absolutely right for the bank.'

I flushed and walked out past them. I could tell they were worried in case I'd overheard anything. I wanted to reassure them I hadn't, so I smiled, and whistled 'Gymnas-ium'.

I told Echo what I'd heard. He was utterly unsurprised. Assuming Nico even wanted us along as bellhops and ballboys and we actually made it to America, we'd all be in for 'a good drubbin''. He reckoned we would get there, though, so long as we kept her needs first. Priority Nico. If she was a hasbeen, then we were never-will-bes, and we had to keep our heads down, just as we had to keep her high. So high that she could maintain her distance from us emotionally and soar away from us in performance on stage every night. We had to stay part of her connection, as Echo said.

'When yer purrit all tergether, what must she get, every time? Scag. That's all she wants.'

'It's all you seem to want, too,' I said.

'She gets the gear, we get the gig . . . an' if there's a bonus from the boss on the night, all well an' good.'

'Boss?'

'Boss.'

Bags

By some freak mischance on his part, Bags ballooned down on us, but he soon bounced back up again.

Bags was Demetrius's protégé. The Doctor was raising him in his own image and to his own methods. . . . Eat first, then think about paying the band. When Bags and Demetrius waddled into a restaurant chefs would raise their hats and cheer.

Bags had Demetrius's bulk but not his personal stature. Where Demetrius would occasionally take us for a pre-gig meal at some pastel-pink Deco Designer Diner with foliage in tubs, Bags was always sniffing out the whiff of a charcoal-grilled half-pounder snaking its way down the street. Of course, with Demetrius, the money was ours to begin with, but at least it sometimes found its way back to us in his munificence. Bags's life was a solitary feast.

Demetrius had crammed Bags into Nico's flat, along with a

synthesiser duo from Sheffield, two young boys Demetrius had taken under his paternal care, Gary and Barry. One dark, one blond; one rough, one smooth. Something for everyone. The blue-eyed blond was Demetrius's ideal, whereas the Lad appealed more to Bags's fascination with the proletarian. It was important, if one intended to get on in the Pop business, to cultivate an interest, at least for a little while, in the habits and pastimes of one's social inferiors. To feel in touch with the simple rhythm of their lives . . . the beat, as it were.

Gary kept a "pen" in the back yard where a few scraggy chickens would peck out a wormless existence between cracks in the flagstones. In the corner Gary had erected a wire hutch in which he kept the chickens' mortal enemies — two ferrets.

Nico's universe was expanding into ever more perplexing dimensions. When Gary first brought a ferret back, she was fascinated yet bewildered.

'What a cuoorieuse little creature. It's not a caaat . . . and it's not a raaat . . . what is it?' She got friendly with the chickens and would tap on the window. They'd come up to her, heads tilted in that one-eyed foolish way. 'This is Esmeralda,' she'd say, 'isn't she sweeet?' And she'd press her lips against the window and give the uncomprehending bird a kiss.

Demetrius spent nurture time with Bags, introducing him to the ways of command. Ordinarily Bags would have gone into insurance if his feet didn't stink so much. Pop music's the last refuge of the true stinker. All those toxins have to settle somewhere and Bags's trainers housed most of them.

Bags had complete contempt for arty popsters who dared to call themselves 'musicians'. Like Demetrius, he shared the belief that Art Rock was a euphemism for 'pretentious crap played by people who lacked the craftsmanship to write a good song, the skill to play an instrument properly, and the intellectual discipline required to create "serious music"'.

Demetrius and Bags had presided over a new line-up. Toby had some bona-fide paid work and wouldn't be coming. So Demetrius called up the number on a business card given to him by the drummer from the Gentlemen Jivers of Jazz. Suddenly we had some strange guy sitting in the middle of Echo's rehearsal room, with a pair of wire brushes, a tuxedo, and perfect teeth. Echo's crumbling yellow cavities spat venomous pus into his ring of confidence. Nico wanted to know who he was, what he was doing in her group, and why he kept smiling.

Dr Demetrius's musical awareness also convinced him that the American audiences loved English guitar heroes. So he hired Didsbury's very own Spider Mike. Spider did the Townshend Twirl, the Bolan Boogie, the Richards Raunch . . . you name it, he could do it. He made up for me, who couldn't do anything.

We gave it one last shot at a rehearsal. Smiler, the drummer, turned up in a dayglo Hawaiian shirt, pastel-blue slacks and a pair of deck sneakers.

'Does he think he's going on holiday?' Nico asked.

He'd finished it all off with a crisp new haircut. He liked to look well-groomed, he said, and 'I just live for that hour on the stage.' He'd always wanted to go to America. What a great opportunity this was. How much he appreciated Nico's choice of him as the drummer. How he'd do a good job for her. Also he'd heard, in case I was interested, that there were some hot spots in L.A. going for good session men. 'Top rates . . . Best brass.'

Echo and Nico kept disappearing to take shot after shot in the hope that the ghastliness would recede. Spider turned up his amp and went into a History of Riffs. I stuck to playing just one note more or less all the time, shifting only when the harmonic changes absolutely demanded it. In this way I kept myself hidden, tucked in between Echo's bass and Spider Mike's guitar. Never, ever, getting in the way of the vocals.

Every so often Smiler would do a fancy little flurry on the snare, or a jazzy rim shot. Nico would slump a bit further on her stool, completely thrown.

Spider Mike dangled just above Smiler. Spinning his web around Nico, buying her drinks with money he'd borrowed from me. His meanness was the only legend that preceded him – but no one had told me. That lugubrious hound-dog face with the permanent drip of snot hanging at the end of his nose. He'd made it quite plain that he loathed me, as he did anyone who had brushed up against the soft-bellied South. I was an over-educated middle-class twat, except 'Twat!' was all he could spare . . . he was a word miser as well. He openly flirted with Nico: 'Aaright swee'heart?' Then he'd wink and put his arm around her. She'd look confused. 'Do you think it's sexual?' she'd ask me later. On the sliding scale of contempt I'd suddenly moved up a couple of notches – above Spider Mike and Smiler, below Demetrius and Echo, at the exact halfway point between Hate and Need . . . Indifference.

BREAKFAST AT PINKVILLE

Detour Ahead: the New York show had been postponed until the end of the tour. It was felt to be more 'appropriate' – in other words there were no punters. It was July. Baking hot. The streets were stinking and melting and full of crazies. Who in their right mind would want to go out? Or punish their ears in some sweltering basement club? Easier to stay home, in the shower, except the waterbugs were waiting.

Detroit

It was straight into action without the usual soundcheck fore-play. We hadn't even seen the hired equipment yet. Bags set up the harmonium – that was the first useful thing we'd seen him do. The dormant instrument had a compact simplicity, like a deckchair – but one that would unfold into a logistical riddle in the hands of the uninitiated. With his backside mooning the already assembled audience of teeth-grinding speed-freaks and rock 'n' roll loners, Bags would get the harmonium to stand freely for a few seconds; then, as he straightened up to leave, it would start to sway mournfully and slowly collapse in upon itself, playing dead. Bags's parka hood would flop over his head as he repeatedly fought the innate guile of his ancient adversary.

We dragged ourselves on stage, still giddy from the turbulence we'd met coming in to land. The organ that had been hired for the tour turned out to be an electric piano, with six keys missing. The game was up. Nico kept turning round and glaring at me during the set – every so often she'd hear the chimey, effete little 'ching' coming from the piano. There was nowhere to hide any more. It meant I would have to listen to Spider Mike and learn his guitar parts, try and double up on the chords. When he went 'chang' I'd go 'ching'. Maybe no one would notice me then. The drummer was still pattering around with the fancy brushwork, like a French pastry chef. Echo had numbed himself out with a swig of methadone. He'd picked up an effects pedal before we left, called a Flanger. It made a weird swishing sound, like the sea rushing over pebbles. He'd play a string and it would resonate on and on over Brighton beach. It meant there was enough space for him to nod out between notes. Boom – woosh – woosh – zzzzz.

Spider Mike was cartwheeling away. I'd catch him on the downstroke (chang/ching). It worked. Nico stopped scowling.

We raced through the seven, then left it to her. Since there were only about thirty people in the audience she wouldn't be treating them to an extensive rendition of the Nico oeuvre. Just enough to make sure we were within the limits of the contract. Not a minute, not a bar, not a stretched melisma more.

After the show a kid strolled up and introduced himself. He was going to be our roadie for the tour. He couldn't have been more than about eighteen. He wore the regulation ripped Cramps T-shirt, combat trousers and army boots. He looked like he'd wasted ten villages single-handed back in 'Nam. His neck was the circumference of Echo's entire body. His skin was tanned by months of survival training out in the Mojave desert. His hair was a square-rigged, regulation military cut. His name was Axel. Echo and I watched him while he single-handedly dismembered the entire stage equipment.

'Army brat . . . probably responds ter discipline,' said Echo menacingly. 'Best not wind 'im up with too much Oxford, Jim.'

Axel picked up the flight-cases and heaved them off the stage, wiping the sweat off his forehead with a red bandana. Real Oliver Stone material.

It turned out his father was a Brigadier-General in the U.S. Marines. Axel, it seemed, had rejected his father's vocation while still retaining the habits of a military upbringing. He approached everything as if it was a dawn raid on Charlie . . . breakfast at Pinkville. He was to be our travelling companion for the next six weeks.

Echo was measuring out a dose of the green syrupy methadone for Nico. 'There yer go . . . the elixir of 'appiness, the nectar of narcosis.'

She slugged it in one. 'That drummer . . . what's his name? He looks at me, like a monkey.'

'Simian,' I said.

'Simon?' she said. 'I thought it was Mick, or Dick.'

'But what about this Axel?' I hoped she could be persuaded to divest us of his already overbearing presence.

'He's very handsome,' she said, suddenly coquettish.

'It's the methadone, Nico,' Echo explained. 'Once yer back on scag yer won't feel so much of the urge within.'

'He has big aaarms, and a tattoooo . . . should I say something to him?' she giggled.

'Like what?' asked Echo.

'Like . . . you know . . . that I find him attraaaactiff.'

'I think yer should tell 'im we need some scag, terribly urgent-like.'

'I had a period this morning . . . I haven't had one of those for years.'

I'd never heard her like this before, discussing biological functions and bodily desires. The black nun was having wicked thoughts and unexpected reminders of that other kind of hunger, need and frustration beyond the end of the needle.

Axel drove us to Chicago to the permanent accompaniment of Metal FM. Muscle was in charge of the brain department – instead of a decent and sensible tour bus he'd turned up in a Chevy four-seater estate, with a trailer hitched on the back. Seven people were about to cross the continent with little else in common except an unfounded faith in the U Haul Trailer company.

Axel had taken it upon himself to be a gung-ho Corporal Peppercorn: 'Yeeah . . . we can do it, guys! Tugether!' and he'd punch the air. He was another idiot in search of adventure, but for him it had to resemble a theatre of war. He'd smirk cockily at other drivers and give them the finger. Charging across lanes, swaying the trailer, so you'd feel the vehicle on the edge of skid all the time, he'd turn the radio up full volume in case any tender shoots of conversation should dare to reveal themselves above the Heavy Metal bombardment. For Axel there was an enemy even greater and more sinister than Communism itself – silence.

Bags the Bulge took the front seat. Four of us squeezed in the back (the temperature was 100 degrees and our bodies were *touching*). Echo found himself a padded crib amongst the luggage. He could string it out to the next dose of methadone so long as he had a place to stretch his aching muscles. His prescription was for two weeks and for himself; Nico seemed to think it was on the tour contract.

Bags dared to twiddle the radio knob. Axel's hand blocked him reflexively: 'Heyyyyy there, buddy – that's my transmission in transition and your omission.'

'Five minutes? Please?' I ventured on everyone's behalf. He ignored me.

'What about a more *pop* station?' suggested Bags, ever the man of the people.

'Hallelujah from the sky — rock 'n' roll will never die.' Axel punched the air again.

'This is ludicrous,' I said, 'there are six other people in this vehicle.'

'Yeeeah, but I'm the driver, Lord Jim – don't you know, where you bin?'

We drove on, with rhyme, without reason.

Chicago

They like the Blues in Chicago . . . Nico's music was so white it was almost translucent. She was indifferent to such *untermensch* basics as rhythm and expression. What we played was like a slap across the face from a Gauleiter's gauntlet. We did a kind of upstairs bar/poolroom. There was no stage. You could hear the balls clacking through her solo spot:

Janitor of Lunacy
Paralyse my infancy
Petrify the empty cradle
Bring hope to them and me.

Clack a tat tat! 'Yo . . . Hey, a couple of beers and some pretzels!'

Two dudes just stood and watched us, leaning on their pool cues, faces impassive, in a kind of sleeping hatred.

Nico still hadn't found a heroin connection and Echo's methadone just wasn't enough. She couldn't get that lift on to the stage without it. So now she was forced to see the boredom and hostility upon the faces of the miserably few punters. Normally the heroin enveloped her, gave her a totality of purpose that propelled her from the dressing-room on to the stage and projected her out towards the audience. It was a substitute for Will.

She had a name in Chicago that she'd been tracking down every spare minute. Finally, just before we left the hotel, she got the address. Axel took some persuading as we had to be in Minneapolis by early evening. She promised him a hit.

We were parked near a vacant lot on the edge of the South Side in our stupid hire car and trailer, like we'd lost the rest of the circus. Nico had picked up the exact whereabouts of her 'friend'. She worked a couple of blocks away.

Axel slowly inched the vehicle along as if it was about to come under sniper fire.

'There she is!' shouted Nico.

There were two women standing on the corner of a tenement block. One had on a pair of ass-splitting hot pants and red thigh boots, the other an off-white minidress and teetering stilettos. There could be no misconception as to their chosen profession.

'Saandra,' Nico leant out of the window.

The girl in the hot pants warily came over. She looked at the car, she looked at the trailer. She wasn't sure. Then she looked at Axel and Bags – she definitely wasn't sure.

Nico called her again from the back. The girl recognised

her and Nico got out. They chatted for a couple of minutes, then walked off. Axel followed up behind.

The girl in the minidress came over. The doors were open for ventilation. She sat herself down in the driver's seat. Her skirt hem 'accidentally' sneaked up to reveal the absence of underwear.

'Twenny bucks a shot, guys, whaddya say? Anyway ya like.'

We tried to pretend we hadn't seen or heard anything, resuming interest in dead conversations and exhausted magazine articles. Though Smiler was giving it some serious consideration, his mouth half-open in that strange Planet of the Apes perma-smile.

The girl fanned herself with her clutch-bag, filling the car with the smell of cheap perfume and stale sex. We all declined:

Out of Moral Prudery – Echo.

Out of Fear of Disease – Me.

Out of Misanthropic Indifference — Spider.

Out of Sudden Loss of Appetite — Bags.

Out of Peer-group Pressure — Smiler.

Cash was tighter than ever after Nico's score, so we had to be prudent with fuel. Axel had a theory that the car burnt significantly less gas if the air-conditioning was switched off. This meant having the windows wide open, though the breeze was baking hot and laden with dust. Later I learnt that this was in fact false economy, the open windows creating a drag effect.

We arrived too late for the Minneapolis show. Now there was even less in the kitty. We had two days to get to Denver, Colorado, on the edge of the Rockies. About eight hundred miles. The only way we could make it was if Nico didn't have to score again, which meant Echo would have to give her the remainder of his methadone. Various ploys were thought up by Axel in order to achieve this, the chief being that we could listen to the radio station of our choice for one hour each day. Echo surrendered his insurance. He'd planned to wean himself off the stuff, but not with quite such an abrupt wrench to the nervous system.

Seven misfits literally stuck together in submission to Axel's military might. 'I want to drive,' Nico shouted. 'Why can't I?'

No one responded. Axel kept his eyes unflinching on the road: 'Rock 'n' roll will never die – you'll never know until you try!' he yelled.

I muttered peevishly from the back, 'Rock 'n' roll is dead and done – bring back Lonnie Donegan.'

'Whassamadda wid Lord Jim? English proper, Oxford prim!'

Nico was catatonic on the methadone: 'That Leonard Cohen . . . he broke my wrist.'

No one had been talking about Leonard Cohen, or wrists. In fact no one was talking at all. Spider Mike had won the toss for a free hour on the radio station of our choice – he chose Zero FM, Radio O.F.F. Perhaps Nico was *making conversation* – but nobody wanted to talk except for drummer-boy Smiler and he was terrified. Every time he opened his mouth, Nico would bite his head off. It wouldn't be anything witty or obtuse, more like 'Shut your fucking monkey face.' But now she was trying to be conciliatory, to sweeten the atmosphere with some idle chitchat. It was the same script she'd been using for years – the events she could recall before she became a junkie and time stood still. Like everyone, Nico had certain landmark experiences in her past, but she never bothered to integrate them into the present. She would only ever quote from her own diary – and that had stopped a decade before.

It seemed unbelievable, but she insisted that she'd never used heroin until after her spell at the Factory. Looming up to her, out of the psychedelic fizz, she'd never noticed anything unusual in anyone's behaviour. She accepted everything. Apart from withdrawal tantrums she hadn't changed. Everything is the way it is. It just happens. The complex skein of historical process was not, one suspects, uppermost in her thoughts.

'. . . he twisted it and twisted it until he broke it.' She was starting to get upset as the memory got closer. The methadone didn't block that stuff out.

Echo came in all conciliatory. 'See what charmin' companions y' ave now, Nico, see 'ow much things've improved.'

She looked about her and yawned. Methadone makes you
sleepy.

It was hard to work out how we came to be pulled for speed-
ing in the middle of Nebraska . . . nothing but prairie-weed
and silence. It meant an on-the-spot cash fine. Everyone
emptied their pockets, except for Nico. That would have
been a bad idea. There was something incriminating in
every crease and crevice of her. Dead needles. Blood-stained
cottons. Bent spoons. The kind of stuff you find in public
toilets.

Another thing I could never work out was why Bags continued to wear his parka jacket as if he was still in Manchester.
Whenever we pulled up for gas and the air was no longer
blasting through, a sweet, all-too-human stink would waft up
from him. It reminded you of school.

We had to curl up somewhere for the night. We tried motel
after motel – they all wanted paying up front. Until we found
Gino's Place. Gino couldn't care less. He only had one room
vacant, every other freeloader loose in America must have been
passing through. He scooped the key off the wall and slapped it
down on the counter.

'Take it or leave it . . . all the same to me, pal.'

We took it. Nico decided she'd rather sleep in the car. That
left six of us in one room. We pulled the double bed apart,
mattress and base – three on each half. Echo and I declined.
Spider Mike and Smiler on one, Bags and his dream companion
Axel on the other. Echo and I huddled in a corner, smoking and
despairing.

By midsummer the American cockroach is well into early
adulthood and in search of a soulmate. And when the lights go
out, he loves to dance *La Cucaracha*. Echo and I weren't
sleeping alone after all. I woke to find my blanket and his
covered in hideous brown bodies. Insect legs had definitely
crawled across my face and woken me up.

'Jesus!' Echo screamed, quietly, as he would. We threw off
our blankets and headed for the car. Nico was laid out on the
back seat, her arms placed in a funereal cross upon her chest.

'What is it?' she said, annoyed at having her place of rest disturbed.

'A plague upon our 'ouse,' said Echo.

Nico tutted. He was talking in sign language again. 'Weell . . . I'm staying here.'

'OK,' we agreed, and sat in the front.

When she was asleep, Echo dipped her bag for the methadone, barely a cupful left. He took a sip, then replaced it. I still had some duty-free Silk Cut. I handed him one, he snapped off the filter and lit up. Nico snored.

Outside the cicadas were singing. The sky was wide open. As far as the eye could see, constellation upon constellation. A silent chorale of stars (the sort of stuff Irish rock groups wax lyrical about).

'I think Tom favours the Tex-Mex style with the side buckles and silver tips. I'm more yer Italian calfskin with elasticated leather vents. Odd as 'ow Cath'lic countries make the best shoes int it?'

'Are you going to talk aaall night through?' asked Nico from behind. 'What with the graaasshoppers . . . and everything . . .'

Echo jumped out and slammed the door behind him. 'Look! We're in the middle of fookin' nowhere, yer've necked all me methadone, so we can do without Germany callin' all night long – right?'

'Shit, you two wouldn't be here without me.'

'An' we're *very* grateful,' Echo hissed through the gaps in his teeth. Nico didn't notice the insincerity.

'OK . . . well, just don't forget it, that's all.'

'We won't, don't you fookin' worry,' said Echo.

Denver

We had big hopes of Denver. Big black-and-yellow butterflies the size of your hand would fly by as you walked down the street, and it wasn't the drugs. Quite why Denver had so many giant butterflies and so many different varieties of drugs, I didn't know, but Echo was chopping out all kinds of curious powders. It seemed to preoccupy his whole attention, choppity-chop-chop, then he'd shovel it with the blade into a neat little square, then choppity-chop-chop again. 'Shall I carve?' Then he'd square up again and divide it into equal halves.

'There yer go, Jim, get summathat down yer.' He swept out a line for me.

'I don't know,' I said nervously. 'It looks a very strange colour to me.'

The sensation was something like having red-hot slivers of glass shoved up your nostrils. 'I can't conceive of the pleasure one might derive from this,' I said to Echo, tears in my eyes and a bitter chemical taste at the back of my throat. I'd been given an original blend of heroin and sulphate: a speedball.

'It might 'elp yer stop bein' such a prick,' he said.

Echo was keen to shove anything up his nose or into his veins, even when obtained from someone more desperate than himself.

Nico was in the toilet with The Monster From Planet Weird circa '68. They were sharing a shot. It was probably a proud moment for him . . . The Queen of the Junkies in his home town. Maybe he'd have the needle framed. It was not inconceivable. People, kids especially, used to ask for her old syringes. Every toilet tells a story.

We did all the favourite turns for the faithful old punters. The people who were so crazy they'd been kicked out of Haight Ashbury fifteen years before. Their brains had burst in the Summer of Love. They'd been shunted further and further inland, and out of sight.

The crazies were the best, though. You'd give them as much high-frequency juice as they could handle. Only the nutters liked us. You began to look forward to them being there. As a unit we were a genetic freak, a hideously deformed, doomed to extinction, limping mongrel of styles. A Happy Hour cocktail drummer. A leaping Guitar Hero. A Penitent Pilgrim of the Poppy. A Fastidious Phony. And King Ludwig's Crazy Sister.

Nico did her famous impersonation of an Alpine foghorn. Smiler just shuffled away with those brushes, dreaming she was Ella Fitzgerald.

'I want to drive . . . I want to drive.' Nico was back on her favourite riff. 'The Velvets used to let me drive,' she said.

'Yeh, but yer used t' drive over people's gardens . . . it's a bit attention-seekin',' said Echo.

'I think I should drive . . . It's not fair, just because I'm . . . you know . . . a gerrl.'

'No it's not,' said Bags from somewhere deep inside his sweltering parka. 'It's because you're a junkie.' The big boy didn't beat about the bush. Bags kept everything on him, there was no point in trying to bust his suitcase – he didn't have one. It was all in that bulging parka. You just knew he had it all stashed – the odd $20 here, the occasional $50 there, creamed off the gigs. They were no-payers but there's always a bit of loose change around. It could add up nicely at the end of twenty dates. Enough to pay for a serious blowout in New York and get photographed with Andy. Bags had decided, one day in the middle of third-year history, that there were the schnorrers at the back drawing naked girls on each other's exercise books, there were the clean-limbed slaves of learning at the front taking down the dates, and there was him in the middle, putting two and two together and waiting for the dinner bell.

We pulled up for gas.

'Can everyone just stay in the goddam car?' said Axel. 'Just sit tight. Every time we fill up you guys shoot off in all directions.'

He went to pay. Everyone got out. Echo went to look for friends that lived under stones. He came back with a small lizard. Nico was sitting behind the wheel.

'It's my turn to drive.'

'We don't take turns,' said Echo. 'We've got a driver, you're the singer, remember?'

'I don't see why I shouldn't drive a little of the way . . .' She was sweating and trembling. The methadone was gone.

'C'mon Nico,' said Bags. 'We've got the Rockies ahead – some dangerous curves and bends.'

She wouldn't let go of the wheel. Echo put the lizard on her shoulder. It ran down her front. She screamed and leapt out of the car. Everyone dived for their regular seats. Business as usual.

We had to put Nico on a flight to L.A. She had friends there who could take care of her habit while we made the big Steinbeck schlepp in our Model T across Nevada, through Death Valley, to the orange groves and the blue Pacific.

Bags briefly removed the parka to reveal a T-shirt that would never be white again. It wasn't just his feet that stank – the whole of him reeked. The parka had merely absorbed the smell. Now we had a big fat cheese in the front seat, sweating and ripening as we drove through one of the hottest places on earth.

We filled up with enough gas to make our crossing of Death Valley, and six plastic packs of ice — the ice cost as much as the petrol. Echo was sweating it out in his crib. He hadn't said a word all day. Spider Mike's face looked meaner than ever — his enormous nose distending into some grotesque baboon-like proboscis. Axel had ripped off all his clothing except for his jockey shorts and combat boots. Bags was already smacking his parched lips at the shimmering mirage of an Olympic-size pool — filled with Italian ice cream. And I could tell Smiler was about to flip — his brains were already scrambled with the heat and the hate from Nico. His smile was now a tight, inflexible grimace that stretched across his face.

Axel thundered on, foot stretched out, the pedal down hard, knuckles white on the wheel. This would be his finest hour.

'Do or die!' He screamed a Rebel Yell.

It was Bags's turn on the radio. But there was nothing to pick up. He tweaked and twitched through the wave-bands; finally he touched on a station. In the distance you could hear it through the crackle of white noise: 'Physical – I wanna get physical/Let me hear your body talk, body talk.'

Silence . . . except for the sound of wheels on hot dust. I turned to check on Echo. He looked dangerously pale, in a foetal crouch, sweating through his shirt. The icepack had melted and fallen from his head. I straightened it for him. His brow felt feverish, his eyes were closed, but his lips were mumbling something. I bent over the seat to listen. Very faintly, from the innermost resources of his trembling lost soul, I could hear the distant trace of The Silver Sweet Siren Song of The Eternal Feminine:

'Ph-physical . . . I wanna g-get ph-physical . . .'

Salvation Sister

Echo was recuperating in the shade of his room at the Tropicana. Every so often he'd peek through the drapes in the hope of spotting Tom Waits, declining to stray outside. After the experience of withdrawals in Death Valley he'd had enough intense experiences for a while. He was fairly straight by now and therefore in low spirits. His guilty past was creeping up on him. Recovering from heroin dependence puts you back in touch with sex. Echo was extremely disconcerted by the unannounced erections he'd begun to experience. He was further mortified by the sudden appearance of four girls cavorting naked in the pool, plus cameraman and director. They were adding the final touches to a searing, post-*noir* exploration into the dark underbelly of Hollywood subculture: *Planet Pussy*.

We had a few days to kill before the first show. Needless to say we were penniless and of course there was nowhere to go anyway. Just setting foot out of the lobby dumped you in another reality where limbs were redundant. You even needed a car to cross the street, no concessions whatsoever were made to pedestrianism.

Nico was staying with some long-time-no-see pals from the good old days of Vaudeville up in Beverly Hills. People who weren't obliged to share their pool with porno starlets. Big Boy Bags and his playmate, Axel, had taken the car and gone off to join her for the day. Echo and I just mooched around his room talking about food.

Bags and Axel turned up in the early evening. They looked edgy, feigning politesse, coked-up, struggling to be straight.

'We guessed you guys might be hungry,' said Axel. 'So look what we gotya.' He held out a paper carrier. Echo took it. Inside were some folded paper napkins, each containing bits of dead food . . . a chicken carcass with a few shreds of meat left on it, a few dried and disillusioned curls of smoked salmon, a

couple of mange-tout peas, squashed *petits fours*, a disinte-
grated cake, and a quarter bottle of Californian Sancerre. Echo
and I looked down at this decomposing corpse of a dinner
party.

'How can we possibly begin to express our gratitude?' I
said. 'That you should even find time in your busy schedule
to consider our needs . . . it really is a mark of true
professionalism.'

'Hey, Lord Jim. No sweat/We done got all that we could
get.'

Nico showed up in a Rolls Royce. A uniformed chauffeur
unceremoniously yanked her out, supporting her as she staggered through the lobby. It turned out someone had introduced
her to the Big Dipper ride through Hell that is Angel Dust. That
stuff has nothing to do with 'getting high' – instead it trans-
forms the user into an android with a vice-like grip and a
mission to search and destroy. Every drug burns off precious
and finite psychic energy. Depending on the chemical agent, it
can be an hour, a day, or even a week – Angel Dust should be
kept in cremation urns.

Nico suddenly looked so old. Her skin hung from her
bones. Later she recounted some of the experience to us. 'It was
like being in the Electric Chair.' She'd even broken some of her
teeth.

'Good job yer got a good dinner down yer before'and,' said
Echo, nodding towards the debris.

There was a certain kind of person who thought it would be
cool to share a drug with Nico. Or introduce her to a new one.
It would make a good celebrity story. And Nico was something
of a celebrity in narcotic circles. Queen of the Junkies. She was
famous within a limited milieu, i.e. heroin users and those who
thought self-destruction a romantic vocation.

Porno-pool life continued unabated. Each day the girls
would arrive dressed like aerobics instructors, electric-blue
spandex leotards and pink tank tops. Half an hour later they'd
be leaping around with spurting hose-pipes, dressed in black
PVC G-strings and garter belts. Echo still couldn't bear to leave
his room, the sexual 'jiggery-pokery' disturbed him so much.

But he still spent all his time peering out from the corner of his window. He maintained he was actually looking out for Tom Waits. 'I reckon sex is best left ter the professionals.'

We were to play our first L.A. show at the Whiskey-A-Go-Go. It was supposed to be the last night of the club's existence. Perhaps the management thought Nico would provide the appropriate funereal solemnity. It was a decent-sized crowd. Except when I asked around, it turned out most of them had come to see the support act, an all-girl Japanese American beat combo in miniskirts and black and white Rickenbackers. After watching them for five minutes it became clear that our musical styles were incompatible. Not only were they sexier than we were, they had some great tunes and an irresistible beat. Surf City was going to love Neolitha the Moon Goddess and her ancient harmonium wheezing out centuries of middle-European angst.

That interminable solo spot of Nico's was like being trapped nightly in some endless time tunnel. We only did seven songs but Spider Mike decided we should keep three for the end. It felt like a dog returning to its vomit.

We exhumed the Grave Raves: 'Femme Fatale', 'All Tomorrow's Parties', 'I'm Waiting for the Man'. L.A. hadn't liked the Velvet Underground the first time around, let alone the cabaret version. It just wasn't their kind of beat. They were another tribe.

I was on their side. When they booed, I booed silently with them. When they heckled, I yearned to make some wisecrack in unison. I wanted to be out there, throwing vodka daiquiris as well. No matter how fast you shovel it, shit always stinks.

Echo cranked up his volume: Boom whoosh whoosh. There it was again — a tide of distortion that drowned out our puny cabaret angst. I prayed it might keep the punters from doing us in. At least it would remind them of the beach.

Inside Echo's suitcase : a satin shirt in deep red. A small mound of indeterminate black underwear. A Bible. A snowstorm of Milan Cathedral. A photograph of The Venus of the Fireplace. A belt with a broken buckle. A sketch book with PRIVATE written on the cover. And six pairs of Italian shoes, all stolen.

'Feel that inner sole . . . cushioned with a veneer of finest calf-skin.'

I felt it.

'Yer won't get that on Oldham market, young Jim.' He held it up to the gaze like a buccaneer showing off a prize ruby. 'A good-lookin' pair of 'ow d'yerdo's – yer can go anywhere. No?'

Blue sky. Blue pool. Blue movie. Echo and I whine in our kennel . . . underdogs scratching each other's fleas.

Spider Mike, it seemed, harboured in his bosom a hidden yearning to meet Bob Dylan. It had been his secret motive for joining up in the first place. He kept asking Nico if she could arrange a meeting, but even Bob Dylan didn't know where Bob Dylan was, let alone Nico, who hadn't seen him in years.

'Bawb encouraged me to sing, you know [5 seconds] he was sweet on me, and I on him [10 seconds]. The others didn't really like him – they were kind of snooooty [2 minutes]. I think they were jalous [30 seconds]. I mean, it took a whole group of them to come up with their little something, no? [10 seconds] Bawb did it all on his own [5 minutes]. He was so nervous and quick. Always in a hurry [10 seconds] everyone wanted something from him [20 seconds]. He wrote a song for me, "I'll Keep It With Mine". Do you know it?'

Unfortunately Spider Mike did. He got out his guitar and accompanied her on the chorus, doing the Dylan nose-singing. 'That's a pearl Nico . . . yet another amazing example of your multi-faceted musical history.' He flattered her into including it in the set.

After the first rendition, Echo decided we had to act with 'extreme prejudice' against the song. He bought a couple of waterpistols. As Spider Mike joined her on stage for the Bob 'n Joan routine, we sprayed them from the wings. It seemed childish, but it was horrible to listen to. It insulted the past, and some of us were still in love with that girl on the cover of Bringing It All Back Home, even if 'Bawb' wasn't.

I chaperoned Echo to the reception desk. Ding!

''as Mr Waits checked in recently?' Echo asked the desk manager.

'Waits?' He ran through the book. 'No. We don't seem to have anyone of that name with us at the moment.'

'Are yer sure?' said Echo. 'Tom Waits, the entertainer.'

'Sorry . . . maybe he was a guest of the previous management. The chiefs changed hats a month ago – new staff, including myself.'

Saxophones were playing slow, sad lowlife serenades in Heartbreak Motel. Echo sloped off to 'knock on Nico's door'. The shoes would remain unsung.

I knew it was a bad idea to remind the Tropicana management of our continued presence in their establishment. They kicked us out. Echo was relieved in a way to abandon the ghost of his absent hero and was consoled, to a degree, by a complimentary unedited copy of *Planet Pussy*. Nico was shunted off to another fan's sofabed. The rest of us spent the night at a friend of Axel's in East L.A., near Boyle Heights – a barrio shack with hungry dogs straining at the end of tethers, rabid jaws salivating for a taste of those gringo sweetbreads.

In the back they were having a barbecue, the top of an old oildrum converted into a brazier. It was hot, sticky, I took off my leather jacket. Immediately a Mexican guy picked it up and tried it on for size, I didn't dare argue. Luckily it didn't fit.

The place was owned by a girl called Rosa. She showed us around indoors. Everything was black – a black shack. Promptly and proudly, she revealed her bedroom, dominated by a black rubber waterbed. On the walls were various hooks and rings from which dangled an intricate assortment of whips and manacles. Rosa was about five foot ten with waist-length black hair and powerful tattooed arms. She looked as if she worked out regularly . . . on other people.

Later, after the nerve-wracking barbecue, in which the Hispanic guys refused to speak English, confining us to a corner huddle of English wimpishness, we found a patch of bare board to call our own in the living-room. In the half light of early dawn amid snores and farts and Bags's stinking feet, I heard Rosa's door open. I sneaked a look and saw her standing over Echo, staring intently at her sleeping prey. She was wearing a black leather corset encased in a breastplate of twisting metal rosebranches with fierce steel thorns. Echo awoke but remained where he was, paralysed. Rosa knelt down, slid her arms under his passive torso, lifted him up lifeless from the cross and carried him to her Chapel of Correction.

The last thing anyone heard of them for twelve hours was the locks on Rosa's bedroom door click shut . . . one by one by one.

''Ave yer ever 'ad an enema?' Echo asked me. 'It gives yer a 'ard-on the size of a baby's arm.'

We were driving along Big Sur. Strange sea-plants, mist, Kerouac, Ansel Adams, and a baby's arm.

'Have you ever read *On the Road*?' Nico asked me.

'No.'

'Neither have I. I couldn't finish it . . . too many woords.' She drifted back into the mist.

'It stays up fer *'ours*,' Echo continued.

Bags wriggled in his seat to accommodate his emergent stiffy. He could whip up some cream right now.

'Did you hear that, Axel?' Nico asked. 'Up for hooours.'

Axel was beginning to get a little less self-confident. Two people in the car had serious designs upon his body, and they were making their intentions abundantly clear.

Nico was in one of her weird, slightly hysterical moods, just on the edge of withdrawal. 'My father was Turkish . . . you know what that means, Axel, don't you? I like it the Turkish way . . . Axel . . . did you hear?'

He didn't respond.

''Ear that, Axel?' said Echo. 'She prefers the tradesman's entrance.'

Axel turned up the Twisted Sister.

Echo fell back into reverie. Further down the road he

nudged me. Through the window the sign read: Welcome to Santa Rosa.

Later Nico picked up some good clean heroin. She soon got Echo fixed up tight with his habit again. It wasn't an act of kindness, she just got sick of Public Enema No 1.

We pulled up for provisions in Redwood country. The truck-stop was a log cabin and there was a picnicky, jolly atmosphere to the place. We could hear children's voices. At the side of the log cabin was a play area.

'Hi there!' said a voice. 'I'm Ronnie, the Redwood Mouse.'

We turned round. There was a giant mouse talking down to us. It must have been ten feet high, the guy inside operating some sort of stilt device.

'And what brings you to Giant Sequoia country?'

'We're musicians, on tour,' said Smiler, teeth ablaze.

'Oh, reeaally?' the voice was slightly camp. 'Are you a group? Who are you?' The mouse was getting excited.

'We're in the Nico band . . .'

Ronnie wouldn't let him finish. 'Oooh – I don't belieeeeve you . . . not Nico of the Velvetth?' The mouse had a lisp. 'But where is sheee? I thimply mutht thpeak to her.'

This could be an exchange of historical significance. Nico came out of the store carrying a carton of Chocomilk. Echo pointed her out to Ronnie.

'That's 'er, in the pilot glasses.'

'Hoooeeeee, Nico!'

She came over and stood before the mighty mouse in her boots and leathers, clutching her Chocomilk.

'Thaaay, Nico, I'm your number one fan. I just luuve *Desert Shore* and *The Marble Index*. I wish I had them here with me now, tho you could thign them.'

'Can you read and write as well?' asked Nico.

'Heeey, Thweetie, I'm not a real mouse.'

'I knooow,' she laughed.

We left them in complete accord. In rodent Ronnie, Nico had, at last, found someone who was genuinely interested in the future of her career.

Wrong Side of the Salt

By the Great Salt Lake was a vast grey mudflat, covered in fat black flies. God knows what they fed on in the alluvial slime – the lake itself was dead. They flew up into your face with each step. By the lake was a funfair . . . a kind of water-chute that looked like a tunnel of plastic dustbins, and a bouncy castle. Children were playing in the mud, making mudpies and mud-castles. The flies soon covered their work, a buzzing tide of disgusting little black bodies.

It was so flat, so lonely, so far away from anything beautiful. These were poor people and this was their beach, a thousand miles from the sea.

Salt Lake City had the best thrift stores in America, yet the most monotonously dressed people. It made no sense. 'This is the place!' Brigham Young had declared, settling on a flyblown mudflat for his New Jerusalem.

We met a nice waitress in a diner on the outskirts of town. She begged us to let her come with us to New York. Perhaps we'd been putting on too much of the phony English charm. She was desperate, though. We explained what kind of vehicle we were in. Not really intended for individual comfort and privacy. It was a heck of a shame, but this was a rough, tough, man's kinda job.

'Tougher'n Duke's saddle,' said Axel. She didn't mind, she'd still come.

We slipped out quietly, mustering the best tip we could for her. On the way back to the car, Spider excused himself. He needed a piss. I watched him walk past our table, scoop up the shrapnel of cents and dimes and disappear into the WC.

'THE KINGDOM OF HEAVEN AWAITS THE PURE IN HEART' said the scripture board on Highway 80 as we limped penitently back across the continent.

It's Up to Yooooo

Bags leapt out from under his parka, came out from his fetid shoe-box and exposed to the world his most latent desire — to meet Andy Warhol. Bags was bugging Nico for an intro, but the

Great Wigola was unavailable, out of town, not answering, reticent as ever. Art object or full-frontal lobotomy? Keep 'em guessing. Bags wanted some business tips.

'Say you want the address of his wig-maker,' I suggested.

'Ask 'im if 'e'll sign me,' added Echo.

Nico told us she wanted to be dropped on the Lower East Side. She made it clear that we wouldn't be welcome tagging along. Echo believed she would probably try to pull in some of her old muso-pals and dump us. 'Can't blame 'er . . . anyone 'ere's better than us, even them spotty kids tryin' out Strats in the music shops.'

Well, she didn't get rid of us. Maybe she was too preoccupied with getting high. However, she had, in the two days that preceded the gig at the Danceteria, been working on a demo of 'New York, New York', Ol' Blue Eyes's eulogy to the Great Meritocracy, with which she would prelude the show.

The Danceteria pulled a good crowd for a sweltering August night. The freaks were in town. Backstage Axel had finally got himself well and truly greased. After six weeks on tour with Nico he'd got the taste and didn't mind the bad taste. He looked green and queasy.

'You shouldn't swallow,' said Nico pitilessly.

The lights went down. On came the tape. Nico lugubriously intoned: 'Start spreading the noos/I'm leaving toooday . . .'

We followed her 'vagabond shoes' up the spiral staircase to our appointment with Destiny.

'It's up to yoooooo/Nooooo York/Nooooo York.'

It was so hot up there, nerves just melted away in the effort to breathe. No matter where it is, if you're playing up close to people, there's always someone who tries to blow your cool. They're there to outface you – and why not? My tormentor stood just three feet away from me with pierced nipples, long blonde hair, lipstick, and was covered head to toe in gold body-paint. He fixed me with a relentless, empty, mannequin-like stare. Weirder still, he had on a Walkman. He looked like a transvestite cybernaut.

I could feel a smile cracking the expressionless mugshot I'd been perfecting. I tried to suppress it so hard I thought I was going to faint. But it was useless. I could blame it on the weeks of contained hysteria and enforced intimacy with people I'd normally pay to avoid. Whatever the reason, I was pissing my pants. I had to stop playing. I turned and saw the drummer beaming the inane grin of a man happy at his work. I was biting my hand in an effort to find a pain substitute for laughter. Echo saw me. He started laughing. Boom, woosh – woosh. Spider Mike took a look at us and had to turn the other way again to conceal the irrepressible smirk creeping across his sourpuss face. Then Nico caught it, in the middle of 'I'm Waiting for the Man':

> I'm ....
> *Chugga chugga chugga chugga*
> .... - - - - - - - / - - - / - -
> *Chikka chikka chikka chikka*
> - - - ....
> *Chugga chugga chugga chugga*
> .... - - / - - - - - - - / - - / my
> *Chikka chikka chikka chikka*
> - - - - / ....
> *Chugga chugga chugga chugga*
> ....26 dollars? ....You must be kidding!
> *Chikka chikka chikka chikka*
> [Permission to reproduce lyrics refused]

She stopped singing, clipped the mike back on to the stand, and turned to the four of us. She was clapping her hands and stomping her heels, like a flamenco Brünnhilde. And laughing, laughing, laughing.

Outside in the street lay a Viking burial. Axel had literally torn the car apart with his hands and then set fire to the remains, releasing the handbrake as it rolled off into SoHo.

We gazed silently at the smouldering wreckage for a few minutes, said our respects, and split. We couldn't wait to get away from each other.

Nico disappeared into the arms of the past, Lower East Side cronies who'd share a bit of stuff with her just for the anecdote value.

Echo headed straight for the shooting galleries of the Bronx. 'Yer walk in . . . it's pitch black . . . yer shout yer order . . . they lower a bucket . . . yer drop in the ackers . . . the bucket comes back a minute later with an 'alf g wrap . . . convenience shoppin' I s'pose, takes the waitin' out of wantin' . . . Tho' I've never been much of what yer might call a shop-a-'olic.'

Bags bought himself a brand new pair of Big Boy jeans with six-inch turnups and then whirled away on a helicopter tour of the Manhattan skyline. Once he'd sized the place up, he took his meat on down the street . . . a cruise missile in 42″ Levis. Like his idol, his art was his life. But still Andy wouldn't pick up the phone.

Spider Mike took the first available flight back to Manchester, disillusioned with the American Way. Now no one back home at the Old Cock would stand him a pint as he traded anecdotes about the legendary meeting between Spider Mike and the only man on the planet he'd ever buy a drink – Lonesome Bob.

Smiler? We asked around next day. No one was sure . . . we heard later he'd gone to New Orleans with a beautiful dancer and was ripping up the rhythm every night, playing drums in a swing outfit, earning 'best brass'. I had a feeling he might come out ahead – he didn't take drugs and wore a clean and pressed pair of slacks every day.

'It's funny,' said Echo on the return flight, ''ow yer think that someone's just a phase in your life – when yer might just be a phase in theirs.'

'ZE CARNEGIE 'ALL'

I never earned a cent from the American tour. Demetrius deferred all responsibility to 'our mutual patroness, Frau Christa Paffgen', who, of course, pointed me straight back to Demetrius. He explained that I should be satisfied with getting such interesting 'trips out'.

It transpired that the promoter had actually tried to be decent and had sent some of our back pay to England. The good doctor had immediately spent it on whores and roulette.

We were back on Echo's sofa. Cheese and pickle sandwiches. Endless brews of PG Tips, percolating grievances. The goldfish had died and been replaced by a tank of pondwater and some black snails. More significantly, the Venus of the Fireplace had been removed and in its place was a picture of the Virgin of Fatima, swathed in rosary beads.

Nico had a piece of opium the size of a Hershey Bar. She was now on first-name terms with every witchdoctor in town. They were happy to do business with her . . . and Demetrius loved to indulge her. To gain the affections of one so wicked and heartless was reward in itself. Nico, of course, continued to abuse him behind his back.

'Thinks he's the big impresario, strutting around like that, while I play provincial toilets.'

Le Kid chirped in, 'Yezz . . . my muzzerre should play ze Carnegie 'All.'

We had Germany and France united once more against the Common Enemy. Le Kid had innate pedigree and, after all, he'd grown up in the company of the Beautiful People — he could do without humiliating handouts.

''Ee is so voolguerre – really.'

Demetrius and the children returned with some friends for the snails. Each of them carried a plastic bag of water with a fish in it. They were like fancy finned goldfish, but black.

'More dependants,' lamented Echo wearily.

Ari went into flip city. 'Zat you spend all ze time in frivolité and my muzerre 'as no monnaie.'

Demetrius pointed out that if Nico chose to spend her income on drugs instead of food and rent like normal people, that was her choice – and not his responsibility.

'The Miseries – why don't you just damn well cheer up? Ask yourselves what spiritual and moral right you have to sit around all day denigrating the efforts of people who at least try to do *something*.'

I went to the bathroom to escape for a minute and clear my head. There were three fish in the sink. I closed the toilet seat, sat down and lit a cigarette. My hands were shaking. Nico started to bang on the door.

'Hurry up, Jim, pleeeease.'

I let her in. She immediately got out her toolbox and arranged her works – all the refinements, the lemon, the candle. It was a genteel diversion for a middle-aged spinster lady, a bit like needlepoint.

I picked something up . . . Echo's methadone bottle. On the label was a warning: 'Keep In A Safe Place Away From Children.'

May '84:
A TUESDAY NIGHT IN PARADISE

Nico was listening to Chopin and eating chocolate. Candle
burning in a saucer, coloured scarf draped over bedside lamp.
Smell of paraffin wax, Marlboro smoke and cooked heroin.

'You want some chocolate?' she asked.

'No thanks . . . it gives me spots.'

'Good . . . then I can squeeze them for you.'

She tutted away to herself: 'Look, he keeps giving me
poems.' She nodded in the direction of the next room.
Demetrius's room. 'Look . . .' She handed me a piece of hotel
stationery; on it was written in manic, spiky handwriting:

> Museum Hotel, Amsterdam
> *Omega*
> I, who, neurasthenic, trembling,
> Yarmulka atop my prematurely bald adolescent crown,
> Convey Mrs Rabinowitz and Aunty Rene
> In auto-erotic Escortina
> To Cousin Naomi for tea,
> Am the same He
> Who stands before thee, erect,
> Upon this wild and foaming shore,
> Where spermatozoic dolphins crest the libidinous
>   waves
> That repeat and repeat evermore:
> Omega. Omega.

I gave it back to her.

'What do you think?' she asked.

'From a literary point of view?'

'No, no, no,' she tutted again, 'What do you think, that he should do such a thing? That he puts this stuff under the door?' She threw the sheet of paper contemptuously across the bed. 'You know he calls to me like a *wiiild aanimal* from his bedroom.' She imitated him, her voice booming even lower: 'Neee-co! Neee-co! I don't answer him. He asks me what I think of his poems, but I know what he *reeeally* wants . . . it drives me craaaazy! Pestering me like some teenager.'

'I think he's got a crush on you,' I said.

'Jesus, you're not kidding. D'you know what he does? In the middle of the night?'

'No.' But I could guess.

'Slap. Slap. Slap . . . I can hear everything, these walls are like paper.' She turned up the Chopin.

I noticed a pile of used disposable hypodermics on the bedside cabinet. She went through them fast. It's hard to imagine that sharp metal bursting through the thin walls of a vein could become blunt so quickly. She didn't have many accessible veins left. They were becoming harder to find, collapsing (or cowering) beneath the surface of the skin. Now she was injecting into her hands – a very conspicuous act for a celebrity junkie. She would cover up her scars with bits of rag, especially if the audience was close to the stage. When you're the wrong side of forty you want to be left alone to get on with it, your habits are your own. They pay to hear the songs, that's enough, surely?

'Don't you ever get lonely?' I asked her suddenly. She didn't seem disconcerted, but thought for a moment.

'Sometimes, when there's not enough youknowwhat,' she laughed. 'But even before that things start coming back at you.'

'Like what?'

'Oh . . . all the *bad* things you've done, all the bad things that happened *to* you. It comes back . . . like a riot . . . the heroin calms me down.'

'Maybe if you had someone, someone special? Perhaps you wouldn't need it so much?'

'I'm OK.' She stopped, thought about it. 'We-ell, maybe a rich doctor who could get me the hundred per cent pure stuff.' She turned over the tape. 'Have you ever been to the desert?' she asked. 'Oh, sure, I forgot, you were in Death Valley. I wish I'd been there with you.'

'You say that now . . .'

'I was in the Sa-haaara, making a film. Loneliness is not so bad when you expect it . . . but when there's lots of people around you don't want, that's lo-onely.'

'I know, there's nothing more depressing than watching other people having fun.'

'And the silence . . . You could shout and shout and no one would bother you, because no one could hear you . . . woooon-derful! D'you know how good it feels just to *shout*?'

'You do that on stage, every night.'

'I guess so . . . but the desert . . . shouting to the emptiness . . . singing the void . . .'

Transmission was fading. 'Don't s'pose you fancy a beer with me and Echo?' I was dry with all that sand. She didn't . . . too tired . . . not so young any more.

I left her to the candlelight, the Chopin and the slap-slap of the 'libidinous waves'.

Devil Shit

We had Gregory Corso along for the ride. Somehow the good Doctor had lassooed him into his care. And Jackie Genova, the Black Crow, Cockney trouble-shooter, who always kept two loaded syringes at the ready in his jacket pocket while driving, so he could shoot at the wheel, eat on the hoof, had come along as Nico's personal dealer. (In the eighties it was the hip thing to bring your own macrobiotic chef on tour with you – Nico always did things differently.)

Jackie made his living by secreting small torpedoes of heroin sealed in condoms in his rectum. He performed a flying doctor service for stricken junkies, forced to make a crash landing in alien territory. When he was a kid, Jackie had worked down the London sewers. Maybe that's why he'd never grown above five foot . . . tender young shoots need plenty of light.

'Awwroyt cocker?' He pulled on the butt end of a Capstan and slapped me on the back. 'Oym your original cheeky Cockney chappie.' He laughed: 'Eeeugh.' It was a kind of reverse laugh, achieved by an inhalation at the back of the throat. It sounded like the dry hinge on a Borstal gate. 'Yore Jim aarncha? Where's the pyshunt?'

He looked like a crow, long beak, black eyes, slicked-back hair. He took me to one side. 'Watch yerself, mate. Ev'ryone of 'em's a cant. Don't let 'em give it and don't you take it. Knowwhamean? Eeeugh.' He creaked his hideous laugh again.

The first thing Corso did was try and get Jackie to take a bag through customs for him: 'Shay,' he lisped through his broken dentures, 'wanchadado me a favour, son, and carry this fer me . . . Bad arthritish . . . Okay?'

Jackie, immediately passed the bag on to Raincoat, who just put it down on the floor.

'Is this someone's bag?' shouted Demetrius. Everyone shrugged.

'So you carry Gregory's bags now,' said Nico, affronted, as they ran the usual gauntlet of customs men.

We played the Lukewarmia type of clubs. The Dutch are the most rock'n'roll-saturated people in Europe. Amsterdam is one big shopping mall on water for druggists and porno-junkies. Groups can't get enough of the brain-scrambling, eye-popping treats on offer. So everyone plays Holland, all the time.

The guys munch gum. The girls zip and unzip their designer flying jackets . . . vampettes with blonde hair and red lips, bored to the back teeth with life at twenty. Their entire aesthetic was built upon a thumb-flick through some style magazine and the first Joy Division album. Only if you set yourself on fire, naked, could you expect even an arched eyebrow. The guys would carry on chewing, occasionally mentioning who they'd seen the night before that was better, who they were going to see at the Milkweig on Saturday that would be better still. We were just Tuesday night at the Paradiso.

Corso came on first. He decided he was going to out-bore

them. He half-recited and half-improvised insults, spraying them with spittle. He'd look over his pince-nez to see if they were wondering who the weird fucker was Jackson-Pollocking them with splatter-verse. I played a bit of free 'plinkety-plonk', as Echo called it, on the piano, which pissed them off even more.

The club in Rotterdam was a true eighties Neo-Constructivist experience, lots of flat colour planes, grey upon grey, with few functional details like people. It was an art-house as doll's house view of culture. Upstairs was an exhibition area. There were lots of things to touch. (As in 'touching is a necessary precondition to cognitive awareness'.) We were going to be taken back to our aquatic foetal past. Art-house as uterus.

Jackie Genova was ahead of me up the stairs. A disembodied voice at the top told him to stop and turn round. He did so. In front of him was a door. 'Come closer,' the anonymous voice said. There were two peep-holes in the door. Jackie hopped forward, the way crows do. 'A little closer,' insisted the voice. He hopped another step. A squirt of yellow piss-coloured liquid shot out at what would ordinarily have been crotch-level but in Jackie's case streaked right across his brand-new La Rocka shirt. A present from his girl.

'*Fackin' cant*!' he screamed. 'Nadine'll go *maaaad*!' He lunged forward with his two index fingers at the peepholes. A pathetic yelping scream came from behind the door, then some crashing and banging as arty Oedipus on the other side was subjected to the severest aesthetic criticism. Exit minus eyes.

Down in the dressing-room it was a veritable symposium. Nico, Corso and Demetrius were comparing ego sizes. Demetrius was quoting Yeats, the poet as Hero. Neither Nico nor Corso seemed in the least bit interested. At the same time the two of them were having problems communicating. Corso was fast, he talked like a Charlie Parker solo, in a nervous flurry of increasingly complex phrases. Nico, on the other hand, preferred the cryptic monosyllable with which she might preoccupy herself for hours. He was nice and polite to her, though, as they did share a certain predilection, and he'd entertained us all with a wonderful Nico parody in the sound check, a rendition of 'When ze Rett Rett Robin/Goes Bawb Bawb Bawbing alongk.'

She didn't take offence, and laughed along with us, so he must have had some charm. He was always a true gentleman with her, in his own decrepit way, and it was good that he was playing scummy clubs as well as the more tasteful POETRY READING TONIGHT snores. He was still a naughty boy. Like Nico, he seemed to be a hotel creature. One canvas holdall, full of personal chaos.

'Demetrius writes poetry too, Gregory,' said Nico.

At the words 'Demetrius/poetry' Echo's ears pricked up like a sleeping pooch. He looked over at me with the dread anticipation of imminent embarrassment in his eyes. Demetrius stood up, placed his Bullworker on the chair:

'Yes, Gregory, I do sometimes indulge in the Homeric art, but perhaps Nico is referring to a particular Elysian elegy of mine concerning a subject of a somewhat more *intimate* nature.' He took a sniff of Vick and tried to sidetrack Nico. 'The downright impertinence of people who inflict their vile cigarette smoke on others appals me, one fears for democracy quite frankly.'

Nico blew her Marlboro smoke in his face. 'Aren't you going to show it to Gregory?'

'No need for that! Poetry should be composed on the wing, off the cuff, is that not so, Grégoire, *mon frère?*' He took off his hat, held it against his chest like a Neopolitan tenor, and gave us a telephone voice recitation of *Omega*.

But when he got to the last line he seemed to go into a strange body-swerve and free-formed a brand-new verse:

> . . . I ejaculate upon
> Your seaweed shore
> I emit my silver testament
> Upon your golden pagan sands
> My Omega!

He synched back into Earth orbit. 'I think you'll agree that in its

central use of the female goddess archetype it resembles somewhat the metaphysical poets, the omnipotent metaphor in
particular.' He looked over at Corso.

'Well . . . if you ashk moy opinion . . . at leasht I ashume
that'sh what you're doing . . . In moy opinion it, ah . . .
shucks.'

'Oh . . . really?' Demetrius was taken aback. It was the first
time in a long while he'd been contradicted by anyone, especially someone who genuinely didn't give a fuck. 'Well at least I
try to confront the nature of the *immortal*, the *eternal*, while
you and your kind merely wish to address the *squalid* and the
unimportant, to rub our noses in the *heathen* slurry.'

'Don't lay that Devil shit on me, man!' screamed Corso,
jumping to his feet and squaring up to Demetrius.

'How undignified!' Demetrius loomed down at him, Big
Telephono. 'Sit down at once, and don't be silly!'

Corso took a swing at him. He missed by a mile. They both
swayed around each other like a couple of hopeless street-
corner drunks . . . a few more shoves and insults. Then they
calmed down. Demetrius was the first to offer his hand.

'Come on, Greg . . . Give me a hug and let's make up like
brothers.'

'Lemmealone, you goddam faggot!' Corso pushed him
away and went aloft to do his routine. After he'd finished, to
the usual patter of tiny palms, Demetrius took the stage. With
his overcoat buttoned up tight, his trilby and his beard, he
looked like a Hassidic Rabbi at a chic Nazi revival meeting:

'. . . And that was my good friend Mr G-r-e-g-o-r-y
C-o-r-s-o-o-o doing some of his bebop poetry for your delec-
tation and amusement . . . Yes, tonight we have a real
Happening for you, boys and girls. In a few moments all the
way from Valhalla, Nico and her Magic Trolls (who've just
popped in from another Nordic saga). T-shirts and posters are
of course available in the foyer . . . and may I add, at a most
reasonable discount for you good people of Amster . . . er,
*Rotter*dam.'

'Get off, you dirty Jew!' shouted a heckler. Demetrius
stopped dead in his tracks. He surveyed the audience.

'OK, which one of you said that? At least have the guts to show yourself.'

Demetrius peered into the darkness but couldn't discern a face, so he decided to take on the whole audience. Give them a real lamming:

'I've seen sheep in fields with shit stuck to their arses that possess more individuality than any of you dumbfuckers.'

A member of the audience applauded him.

'I've seen rollmop herrings that show   more signs of *joie de vivre.'*

The audience cheered and whistled with delight. It was the first time they'd found a laugh at a Nico gig . . . but then they hadn't seen her with the Jolly Boys in tow.

Demetrius stepped into the wings, wiping his bald pate with a firm handkerchief. A mixture of anger and triumph: 'My God, did you catch all that?'

'I certainly did,' I replied, not knowing whether to congratulate or commiserate.

'Really outrageous. They're so far beyond any norms of decency yet,' he paused to catch his breath, 'they're such break-neck conformists.'

I gave him a sip of my Tizer.

'I mean . . .' He foraged inside his overcoat pocket for the bottle of valium and the tube of Vick '. . . it's not as if . . .' gulp, gulp, sniff, sniff . . . 'I even *look* Jewish.'

Since his previous spell of action with Nico's unit, Toby had seen a tour of duty with a Grunge Metal outfit from Wigan and he now sported a wild bush of curly hair. Echo couldn't bear it any longer:

'Is that what yer might call an Afro 'airdo, Toby?'

'Give us a break, mate,' said Toby, stubbing out his Benson butt with his heel.

'A'm not goin' on stage with an extra from *Superfly*. An' 'e's' – pointing to me – 'never out of the fookin' mirror. It's like bein' stuck with a pair of powder-room tarts.'

Really he was looking for any excuse not to have to do the dreaded deed. The bridegroom's fear of the bride.

Toby threw a bottle of Tizer across the room. A fizzy brown Molotov burst against the wall. 'I'm sick of drinkin' fookin' pop.'

'I'm sick of playing fuckin' pop,' I said.

'You wouldn't know 'ow,' hissed Echo. Nico came in and saw the smashed bottle of Tizer.

'Have the poets been fighting again?'

We persuaded Echo to at least come upstairs and play from behind the wing curtain. Raincoat took one look at him: fedora, wrap-round shades, jacket buttoned up collarhigh.

'Dearie me, Mister Misterioso, mucho tremuloso.'

Toby counted us in, but it was pointless, since Echo could neither see nor hear him properly. We usually played a short intro – cabaret-style – then Nico would stride on. This time she waltzed right into Echo, hiding in the wings. There was a 'boom' but no 'woosh, woosh'. They were both freaking at each other. It was just Toby and me up there. One thin organ note and Manchester's loudest drummer.

Then they both came on, Echo still buttoned up, and Nico cursing him under her breath as she took up the mike. She kept turning round to find Echo hiding directly behind me. Whenever I moved, he moved in the same direction, like a shadow dancer.

Echo was supposed to come in on the chorus of 'Femme Fatale'. It had to be semi-sung, in that blank putdown Factory style. We hobbled up to the mike, like some bizarre pantomime horse, I sidestepped at the appropriate moment, Echo closed his eyes, so as not to see the audience. 'She's a . . .' There was only a second's pause, but it seemed to balloon into infinity. '. . . F . . . F . . . OH, FUCK IT.'

'Another proud moment in a distinguished career,' smirked Demetrius later in the dressing-room post-mortem.

Between the two of them, Nico and Corso had blown all the gear. Corso wanted Jackie to do a run for him, and gave him

$200 to get a couple of grams of 'the shame shtuff as you guysh'.

Now there could have been room for misunderstanding here, since at any given moment there was likely to be a bewildering array of substances being snorted, smoked, popped, cooked or cranked. But it was obvious what he was after. When Jackie handed him two grams of coke, Corso was none too happy.

'You goddam little runt . . . I wanted shmack . . . whaddya gimme this shit for?'

Jackie wiped the spittle from his face. 'It's the same gear as wot they 'ave – they're into coke at the minute, squire.'

'What fuckin' good ish coke t'me? You short-assed, pin-brained lil pimp!'

Raincoat had a solution. 'Maybe we could take it off yer 'ands, Gregory – though I don't think we can quite muster the full monte.' He offered him $100 for the lot.

'Jeshus Chrisht, it'sh like being in shome Cairo bazaar with you hustlers.' Corso grabbed the money and flicked the wrap of coke contemptuously across the table.

Raincoat patted his waistcoat pocket. 'Mercy beaucoop notra amigo de Penguin Modern Poets.'

Corso shook his head. You wondered why he bothered. The hustle never stopped. He hung on for a few more days, pestering Demetrius for some sort of fee . . . but the Nico T-shirts weren't selling, nor were the bootleg cassettes and the 'signed' (by Demetrius) albums. Eventually, exasperated by his demands, Demetrius found Corso a refuge with a literary type. 'One junkie's enough,' said Demetrius, firing a warning shot across Echo's bows. Demetrius couldn't quite cross Corso's name from his address book, but future projects were unlikely. Later, he got a postcard from the Master Beat; it simply read: 'Watch your ass!'

Echo had it narrowed down. There was his way of seeing things. All else was 'Ka-ka'.

Nico was Ka-ka, as were her satellites and acolytes.

We were back in Amsterdam, sharing a room that overlooked the Rijksmuseum, which houses the Rembrandts.

'They're all like mud,' he said. 'Walls of Ka-ka . . . I went with Faith . . .'

'But came out disillusioned?' I quipped.

'No . . . with *Faith*.' (He had a horror of puns – they encoded a kind of middle-class unease and college-boy competitiveness.)

Sharing a hotel room with Echo was like doing time in a penitential cell. God knows, there were enough distractions in Amsterdam. We could gawk and gape around the red-light area, or dare to sample the fleeting joys therein? The beautiful, willowy Indonesian girls, maybe that special Professionelle of sterner stuff for him? Hmm? . . . Hmm?

'Ka-ka,' said Echo.

Next night Echo came downstairs with a reel of cable slung over his shoulder. He plugged the jack into his guitar. The other end was attached to his amp on stage. He intended to play the gig from the dressing-room. Toby and I reasoned, Demetrius threatened – to no avail.

Echo resembled the only thing we had that was close to 'cool'. And he'd just fired himself.

Manchester

The fish had eaten the snails and died. Now there was just a lifeless tank with a snowstorm of Milan Cathedral in the middle of it.

I suggested to Echo that he might have curbed his heroin abuse and kept a tighter grip on things musically.

'What d'you fookin' know?'

'I know when to keep my head down.'

'Yeh, you fuckers always do – comes natural to the spineless.'

'I'm sorry?'

'No yer not . . . but yer fookin' well will be, playin' that bag of bollocks . . . spineless . . . yer 'aven't the guts ter drop it.'

'Hold on a second . . . why should I do myself out of the

only gainful employment I've got just because you choose to put down your guitar and take up the needle instead?'

'Yer could always give piano lessons. *A Tune a Day.* I guarantee results.'

As I left I heard the children singing their weird little rhyme again:

> Hark! Hark!
> The dogs do bark!
> The beggars are coming to town.
> One in rags,
> One in jags.
> And one . . .

'. . . in the Velvet Underground,' I muttered to myself, closing the gate behind me.

ÜBER ALLES

Free University, Berlin

In the next dressing-room, the other group was limbering up.

'Hun-a . . . Hun-a . . . Hun-a . . .' Hard-core, leathered-up Teutons. Very *Sturm und Drang* . . . very angry.

Raincoat dunked his teabag. 'Betcher anythin' they've all got day-jobs in a skin shop . . . I know the type – all saddlesoap and no polish.'

Nico chuckled. 'You mean, they're all fa-a-ags?'

'Course they are. All that "Night of the Long Knives" bizness, everyone of 'em a brown 'atter.

Unbelievably, Raincoat was the road manager in Demetrius's absence (fear of flying). Raincoat's chief concern was to ensure a plentiful supply of teabags and jammy dodgers in the dressing-room. And, of course, to assist Nico in any way possible in the acquisition and administration of her personal needs.

'Bosch – Krupp – Bosch – Krupp . . .' The storm troopers were hammering their fists on the wall. Nico had opted to let them go on first – so she could top the bill. It was five or six years since she'd last appeared in Berlin and there was an air of expectancy, at least in our dressing-room.

For a small guy, Echo's absence left a big hole. Demetrius had attempted to fill it with a funk rhythm section from Chorlton, plus Spider Mike on guitar . . . slap bass and the Pinball Wizard. Nico seemed as unconcerned as ever. Either she was prepared to sacrifice her last remaining shreds of credibility by ignoring the musical incompetence of her accompaniment or, in some bizarre hubris, she perhaps imagined that the naked contrast of styles between the 'purity' of her solo spot and the directionless absurdity of her backing would somehow isolate and enhance her true artistic status, like a diamond in a slag-heap. She believed in the 'Star System', that fate confers upon certain chosen individuals a life of higher meaning and purpose. 'Garbo lives in me.' Nico maintained that Garbo's soul trans-migrated to her body when the Nordic goddess retired from the screen.

'Always thought our budgie 'ad a look of Steve McQueen,' said Raincoat.

The audience were in a slavering sulphate frenzy by the time the support group had finished. They wanted *substance*, they wanted *meat*, they wanted to fill their ears with the screams of battle and the clash of steel on steel.

We'd barely got into the first number before a blitzkrieg of beer glasses rained down upon us. Nico shooed us all off stage and told the crew to turn down the lights, leaving one single spot searchlight illuminating the harmonium. She would show them who was boss.

There were a few refractory barks from *Der Jungling* but the beer assault abated. Nico started up the pedals. She began to play a weird, haunting little tune in a major key. Major keys were something of a rarity in Nico's repertoire. I listened from the wings. It was almost like a children's nursery song, curling insidiously around the hall, its nagging simplicity simul-taneously disconcerting and intriguing the audience.

'This song is dedicated to Ulrike Meinhof.' A few cheers. Then she began:

> *Deutschland, Deutschland über alles . . .*
> *Einigkeit und Recht und Freiheit*
> (Unity and Justice and Freedom)
> *Für das Deutsche Vaterland*
> (For the German Fatherland)

'Hitlerite!' someone shouted.

'Nazi!' yelled another. Soon the whole assembly took up the chant: 'Na-zi! Na-zi!'

The first beer bottle glanced off the side of the harmonium.

Nico picked up her cigarettes and set-list. 'Na-zi! Na-zi!' They continued hurling bottles and shouting after her as she left the stage, punching their fists in the air in a perfectly synchronised salutation.

'Jesus. I hate this country,' said Nico afterwards. 'Every time I come here I remember why I left.'

July '84:

BEDSIDE MANNERS & SEASIDE FRIENDS

Paolo Bendini had been a junior chess ace when he was at school. Stalemate with Spassky. But Dr Demetrius was springing a whole new set of openers on him.

'Eees no possible. Eees no possible,' he kept saying.

'Nonsense,' said Demetrius. 'You booked Nico for a tour and here she is.'

'No! No! No! No! No! No! No! I say on the telephone, maybe, *perhaps – No* ees . . . definite . . . Why you are here?'

Why? Because Dr Demetrius needed a holiday where the food was beautiful and the girls delicious.

We were walled up in an ancient hotel in a small north Italian town called Ivrea. The place was a great decaying *torta naziale* with nineteenth-century plumbing that shook the plaster off the bathroom walls. Maybe it had once been grand and busy, but now it was well off the trade route. We'd been there over a week and we were the only guests. The landlady had given up asking for money and just gave us sour looks whenever we came out of the lift.

Demetrius had finally come to an unavoidable conclusion – why bother with the music? Just have the tour. Paolo Bendini, a young Italian promoter, had ventured to hint at the possibility of some forthcoming Nico concerts in the distant future. That was enough for Demetrius. Immediately he hired a van from R & O and filled it with every Girophile he knew.

Toby and Raincoat had come out loaded with crates of Nico T-shirts as insurance. Raincoat had already offloaded dozens of them on to the landlady's family, softening her up with his Esperaincoat, explaining that they were collectors' items: 'Mucho valubile.'

The tour was a stalemate – Demetrius insisting that we'd been booked, Bendini categorically refusing to believe what was happening to him. A vanload of itinerant musos dumped on his doorstep. It was another link in a chain of bad luck he'd been dragging along since he started out. Bendini had ventured into concert promotion through a genuine love of the music. First mistake. He'd just done a Neil Young concert which had bombed out – the middle of July in Rome, 75,000-seater stadium, and it rained. Only for one day, but very specifically and very hard. Paolo was just a small, sweet guy, with pimples and brainbox lenses, an office at home in his bedroom and his mother's ravioli. Now this. Demetrius bullied, cajoled, coerced and confused him until the Bendini head was spinning – figures were floating, contracts were waving. Demetrius had him in check. Bendini would go back to his mum's and try and work something out.

We sat it out for the best part of another week. Nico had a nice little bag of Manchester scag in her pouch, plus her little Joey, Le Kid. They only ever appeared at mealtimes, scuttling back to their room to get loaded. Demetrius hinted at incest, as they shared the same bed – but then they shared the same everything.

It was decided to put on a private concert for the landlady and her family in the hotel basement to keep them all sweet. Demetrius had dropped words like *bel canto* and *coloratura*. The Signora was expecting a few arias from *Rigoletto*.

There was a strange old uncle, deathly thin, with a hat and a walking cane, who haunted the upstairs landings and looked straight through you when you spoke to him. I stayed in my room as much as possible. I'd found a porno cartoon mag on top of the wardrobe: *Leonora the Leopard Lady*. She provided some solace and companionship throughout those interminable siesta hours. Neither waking nor sleeping, I could hear Uncle Morbido creeping about outside. Sometimes I'd notice the handle turn on my door. Maybe Leonora was already spoken for.

Demetrius had commandeered a microphone and a box amp. The harmonium was taken out of its native soil and placed under the one single lightbulb. The cellar looked, appropriately enough, like a torture chamber. Luckily it was to be an exclusive solo performance, for one afternoon only.

It was a packed house. The whole dynasty . . . kids running around like puppies, all wearing Nico T-shirts. Grandma was magnificent, spreading her sombre influence like a black widow spider from the corner of the room.

'*Per me*,' she sighed, '*la bella vita finira presto.*'

Our good landlady and Nico came in arm in arm. Le Kid, high on his mother's dope, followed behind; then the good Doctor and finally old Morbido, who just walked past everybody to the other side of the room and leant against the wall, leaning on his walking stick.

The Signora said a few words about 'what an honour it was', etc, etc, and then Nico began.

'I want to begin with 'The End'. This song was Jim Morrison's favourite song.'

> This is the end,
> Beautiful friend,
> This is the end,
> My only friend, the end
> Of our elaborate plans, the end
> Of everything that stands, the end . . .

It was the perfect family portrait, frozen in time. No one moved. Mouths hung open.

Old Morbido was the first to crack. He began to sway from side to side. Then the dog began to whine. Grandma had seen a glimpse of the Other Side and didn't like it. Some of the younger kids were a bit frightened by the strange lady in black with the man's voice, but the teenies were biting their tongues in an effort to suppress their laughter. Uncle Morbido started to wander around with his stick, banging into things, like he was drunk, blind or delirious. The Signora got a grip of him and marched him off to his familiar haunts upstairs.

Nico called it quits after the one song, and everyone relaxed again. Cakes and Fanta were handed out for the kids and grappa for the adults. Nico didn't seem too put out by the brevity of her recital as she still remained the glamorous centre of attention. What everyone really wanted was a party. So we had one, there in the basement.

Le Kid had taken a fancy to the landlord's beautiful daughter.

'I 'ave 'eard zeese Italian guerrls are good for ze sex.'

'Oh, aye,' said Toby, 'they think of nowt' else. Bred like pedigrees they are.'

'Do you sink I could fuck 'er?'

'With your irresistible Gallic charm, no problem.'

When everyone had loosened up on the grappa, Grannie suggested it was time for more music. It was Raincoat's turn to do a song, and I had to accompany him on the harmonium.

> My funny Valentine,
> Sweet comic Valentine,
> You make me smile with my heart.
> Your looks are laughable,
> Unphotographable,
> But you're my favourite work of art.

He tilted into the full Sinatra croon. Smooching up to the Signora and Grandma. Then he sidled up to Nico and, astoundingly, she took up the final verse. Then together they sang the last lines.

> But don't change a hair for me,
> Not if you care for me,
> Stay, little Valentine, stay –
> Each day is Valentine's day.

The basement went bananas. They wanted more! But we didn't have any more. So it was back to whacking off in our rooms.

It was the best gig we'd ever played.

Down in reception Demetrius was working the Signora's phone to death, pestering Bendini. The bills still hadn't been paid, so we all took to Nico's routine of creeping out of our rooms at the exact moment the evening meal appeared and then disappearing again like ghosts.

Demetrius took me to one side. 'James. I think I'm going to have to close down operations here. No doubt the chaps will be disappointed. But at least they've had a good trip out.'

'So . . . no tour?'

'Wee-eell . . . it might be advisable for one of us to stay on here with Nico, just to await developments.' And then he tipped me a wink. 'Who knows?' he continued, 'it might prove to be quite a profitable experience . . .'

'But what about Raincoat and Toby?'

'They seem to have become imbued with the entrepreneurial spirit and intend to make their fortunes selling Nico T-shirts on the Italian Riviera. They'll rendezvous with you a little later in Milan.'

'And . . . Le Kid?'

'Er . . .'

'You mean Le Kid comes too?'

'Er . . .'

'You know what happens . . . he burns into her stuff and then it's *La Grande Tragédie*.'

'They're inseparable,' said Demetrius. 'Like you say . . . a kangaroo and her Joey hopping round the corner for a fix!' He started hopping like a kangaroo. The Signora glared up from her accounts book.

That night Bendini telephoned to confirm some dates. Short-notice affairs – hard to tell how they'd turn out.

'We'll take it.'

There might not be much money.

'We'll take it.'

Maybe nothing at all after hotels and fuel.

'We'll take it.'

Demetrius clicked down the phone with a broad beam. Checkmate.

Demetrius had some pressing business to attend to back in Manchester but he'd pop back to collect us at the end of the tour.

'Toodle-pip!'

The hotel went deathly quiet after Demetrius's departure. My only human contact was with Nico and Le Kid at feeding time, where they chorused their woes and grievances. Demetrius the Deceiver, Demetrius the Dreamer, Demetrius the Deflowerer of Catholic Virgins.

Lonely, I started to haunt the corridors along with Uncle Morbido. Then Franco showed up.

Franco had been a test driver for Fiat in Turin and a medium-level racing driver. Now he was a 'Records [sic] producer', whatever that meant. He was also a pal of Bendini's, in his mid-thirties, greying, handsome, half Yugoslav, half Italian, and he liked speed (i.e. rapid motion). You'd never have guessed, though, because he talked really slowly and had a quiet, slightly pained, old-world courtesy.

He picked us up in a stripped-down, souped-up old Peugeot Pimpmobile. The kind of thing the Brigate Rosse wire up with a dead judge in the boot. He explained there was going to be a lot of driving, so he just wanted to ride the car to death.

Franco dropped the Signora a wad of lire out of his own pocket. Nico and Le Kid snuggled down in the back, sharing each other's joys and woes. We tore off down the autostrada, making it to Milan in 'Records producer' time.

I knew it was a mistake the moment we arrived at the station. I remembered Echo had warned me about the place before. We were parked illegally at the foot of the steps, looking hopelessly conspicuous. Nico had gone to the WC for a shot. Raincoat and Toby were late. We were three guys in black leather jackets, all smoking, and looking furtively around us for a miracle in Milan.

There was a thump on the roof, then the side doors ripped open and suddenly I was dragged out of the car and told to assume the position while four rifle-toting cops frisked us individually.

'*Stiamo aspetiando degli amici* [We're waiting for some friends],' said Franco.

'*Zitto* [Shut it].'

They finished feeling us up and down and then they started on the car. That wouldn't take long, there wasn't much to pull apart. One of them watched us while the other three tossed our gear on to the pavement. My bag fell open and out leapt *Leonora the Leopard Lady.*

'*Depravato!*' our guard sneered. I blushed guiltily.

'*Maman!*' shouted Le Kid.

Maman was hovering at the back of the crowd.

'*Vieni qui,*' said one of the cops. '*Passaporto?*'

They looked in her bag . . . Stephen King, a lemon, a bottle of grappa, a Nico T-shirt – and that was just the first layer, there was at least a decade of ring-growth to get through. Luckily she had her works and dope in her knickers and I assume they didn't fancy a frisk. To my knowledge she hadn't taken a bath since the last time she was in Milan.

Incredibly, they let us go. Maybe they realised we were just too conspicuously stupid to be a serious terrorist threat.

The beggars, hookers and hustlers all fell back into place.

'Let's get out of here,' said Nico.

'What about Raincoat and Toby?' I ventured.

'Fuck them . . . Franco – presto!'

It felt best and perhaps appropriate to bid farewell to the Leopard Lady there, on the steps of Milan station.

We were on the overnight ferry from Civitavecchia to Sardinia. Bendini had fixed us up with an open air concert in Cagliari. Franco had other business. It was just me, Nico and Le Kid. We'd been talking about her modelling days, about how 'My Funny Valentine' was one of the first songs she ever learnt as a professional singer, and of a cover shot she did for an album by Bill Evans, the jazz pianist, called *Moonbeams.* I told her I couldn't really imagine her in those days, having to get up on time, keeping a fastidious diet. (For the last couple of months back in Manchester her sole diet had been custard. 'So cheap – and not like eating at all.')

'I can see myself just the same then as I am now.'

She was fortunate in this respect. A lot of ex-models find it hard, after living exclusively on their looks, to be suddenly asked to develop a character. One could only ever imagine Nico as a constant, unchanging entity. She wasn't quick on the uptake or particularly fast on the putdown, but she was consistent. It was like she'd always been there in our lives. One couldn't imagine the landscape without her. Sullen, sour, monumental, yet powerful. The solid granite power of an inflexible will. Those boots, those heavy peasant bones, the foghorn voice. Here she comes: Estradella and her Dog of Doom.

The captain announced we were passing the island of Elba, Bonaparte's Alcatraz.

'They were saaadists . . .' she said.

'Who's that?' I asked.

'The English . . . that they should bring him here. From the woorld to a rock.'

Le Kid puffed on his spindly joint. 'Do you sink zey broat 'im guerrls?'

'Probably,' I said, 'along with *Le Figaro* and the latest copy of *Elle* magazine.'

His lips puckered tighter than a tomcat's asshole. I was not being '*sérieux*'. Le Kid had inherited his mother's sense of humour.

When we arrived in Cagliari the local promoter picked us up in his 2CV. He was sweet, a fan. That meant he probably didn't know what he was doing. Nico stole his shades. Bendini turned up; he brought with him his assistant Mario and his secretary Marina. My God, maybe it was the heat, but she had a definite look of Leonora the Leopard Lady. Le Kid broke into a sweat. Instantly he wanted to mate with her and started spraying his scent . . . 'I am Nico's son . . . I was een ze Factory wiz Andee War'ol.' She was going to drive us all crazy.

The hotel had a private beach. We all scuttled down there like nesting turtles. Marina did her stuff – the whole Birth of Aphrodite routine. Only Bendini remained free of the 'libidinous waves'. She jiggled her tits in his face, but the little fellow was so myopic he missed it. The rest of us just ached and dug ourselves deep into the 'pagan sands'.

Maybe fifty people showed up at the gig. A girl in a day-glo swimsuit asked me if I was Nico.

We did a couple more Club 18–30 Nostalgia Nights. Le Kid was petulant and pouting.

'Ze Carnegie 'All . . . ze Carnegie 'All . . . my muzzere should play ze Carnegie 'All.'

Bendini was running around the island sticking up fly posters. They slithered down again before you could read them.

It was the height of Michael Jackson *Thriller* fever. At Klub Kinky the cruel disco heat burnt and blistered our pale Northern European skin. Kids were circling round us, body popping and moonwalking. The lights went down to reveal: Death at the Heart of the Disco. We lasted about ten minutes. They just played a 12-inch megamix of 'Billy Jean' over what we were doing and faded us out.

I got the feeling Bendini had simply phoned up his friends, any friend, who might possess a Nico album, and asked them if they wanted to do some shows. Klub Kinky, Cagliari, was as far away as Nico could ever get from 'Ze Carnegie 'All'. Kidnappers, bandits, donkeys, tourist villages, glazed terracotta tiles, handwoven peasant blankets, coloured rugs, baskets, sun, blue sea, white rocks, sand they had a-plenty, but Billy Jean was not my love. Le Kid was not my son.

Civitavecchia

The harmonium was swaddled in its old blanket, like a refugee's sad bundle. It was Nico's only real possession. Without it she had nothing to trade – even though its bronchial wheeze spelt instant death to the disco children. Nico's songs of mortality and decay were not compatible with the dominant rhythm of the eighties, especially not for honeymoon couples and resort developers.

A swarm of ants was teeming about their insane and remorseless duty at my feet. It was 3.00 p.m. Siesta. The cicadas were chattering and telegraphing their nervous messages to one another. Our backsides were burning on a hot stone bench. Nothing of human intent or design was moving on Civitavecchia station. Except a single, silent tear down the side of Nico's face.

'I guess I'm through,' she said.

I stared down at the ants.

'They want disco music now.'

I put my arm around her shoulder. She was sweating and shuddering. She looked up at the sky, trying to keep back the tears that were brimming in her eyes. This wasn't the familiar withdrawal hysteria I'd seen all too often before. Certainly the smack wasn't coating every nerve and cushioning reality; instead what she was seeing was more than just her misery, what she was feeling was more than her self-pity.

'What can I do? I can't do anything else.'

'You've still got your voice,' I said. 'Can't you write some more songs? You need to make a record – get your face about a bit. It's no good busking around discos hoping to pick up pennies to score. People have got to *want* to see you.'

'I know. I know,' she sighed, weary at the prospect of having to rebuild her derelict career.

'But look,' I said, trying to reassure her, 'it's not like you have to start from nowhere. People don't need to be convinced. It's just . . .' How to put it? '. . . It's just that, well . . . you're bone idle.'

She looked at me, curiously, then laughed. 'I guess you're right . . . Aaandy always said I was laaazy.'

'You should make a record, Nico – then the tours'll have some meaning. You won't need to play seaside discos.'

Le Kid was endlessly making and remaking his one silly little joint with a few meagre crumbs of hash. 'My muzzerre should play –'

I came in on the chorus. 'Don't tell me – 'Ze Carnegie 'All.'

THE SMILE OF A MEDIEVALIST

Suddenly Dr Demetrius began to devote his powers of per-
suasion to something other than tourism. His ultimate goal
was, of course, to secure more tours, but it had become obvious
even to the most dedicated holidaymaker that no one would be
going anywhere until Nico became a going concern.

Nico had tried to run away a number of times after the
Italian disco tour, but no one else really wanted to look after
her. She'd camp out on sofas, stretching her hosts' generosity to
the limits, until they'd have to say or do something hostile. I'd
heard that at the height of Sergeant Pepper mania Paul
McCartney's chief concern was in getting Nico out of his
living-room.

She tried it on everywhere, even my girlfriend's. They got on
like two cats in a sack. At first she'd be charming and sweet and
talking about recipes, and then things would start to turn a mite
strange. For instance, you'd find suggestions and alterations
being made to your TV schedule. Comedy programmes were
bypassed for anything even remotely connected with Death. She
moved on to a friend's place. But when he found all his spoons
had become mysteriously bent and burnt, and his pretty young
wife expressing fascination with Nico's little pochette of pinkish brown powder, he put her on the first available flight to
New York – where she bugged my brother for floor space.

It wasn't that nobody liked Nico. In fact they were, mostly,
very fond of her. But she was a junkie. Junkies, any kind, are
invalids with criminal tendencies. They can't be trusted. It's not

their fault. Their need is greater than they are.

You witness their vulnerability and you want to help because they're your friends or colleagues. But you know they're going to let you down. I'd implored Echo to come and stay with me and sweat it out; wisely he'd turned down the offer. His voice was fainter than ever on the phone:

'Thanks, Jim . . . But what I really need . . . is the stuff.'

He was being honest. Moreover, he knew if he accepted my offer he'd be forced into dishonest behaviour. I think that's why we'd fallen out. I just wasn't prepared to walk the same Via Dolorosa.

But, in order not to succumb, you're forced, as a witness, to harden your will in a manner ultimately injurious to the spirit. I think we all loved Nico. But those of us especially who weren't prepared to sacrifice themselves to smack found it necessary to fix a limit to that affection. And that's unnatural. The way we did it, mostly, was through humour. It wasn't meant to hurt her, more to protect ourselves from her predatory influence.

It reached an insane level, though, when Demetrius conducted an interview on the phone to a music magazine, impersonating Nico. As the journalist got suckered in deeper, Demetrius/Nico got wilder and more fantastic in his claims. The interview closed on a major scoop/revelation, that Andy 'isn't really, well, you know, strictly – "gaay" . . . in fact, we've often shared a very rich and rewarding love life together over the years.'

Number 23 Effra Road, Brixton, was owned by a Mrs Chin, a respectable, church-going, Jamaican landlady who'd married a Chinaman and ran a small grocer's shop down Coldharbour Lane.

The first time Demetrius and I looked over the flat we thought it was perfect, mainly because we liked the two imposing white stone lions on the porch. The place itself consisted of the top two floors of an end-terrace Victorian house.

Many people from the North of England are anxious about living in the unlovely city of London. However, Manchester man that he was, Demetrius had decided, about time, that Nico had to be seen on the scene. She had to get with a solid record company. Manchester was too small and specific. There, you had to be eighteen and living in a squat in Didsbury to qualify, you had to be new. Demetrius had to find a kind person in charge of an approachable record label. (There was no sense at all in talking to the Praetorian Guard of little girls in miniskirts who are employed to repel the advances of any itinerant chancers hoping to score a quick advance.)

We had a look round the flat. Three bedrooms, living-room, kitchen, bathroom. Clean. White. Discreet. Perfect. It was an ideal safe-house from which Dr Demetrius could launch Nico's Teutonic terror campaign on the funky phonies of south London.

He'd had his car fixed up. He'd invested in a new suit from High and Mighty. Big silk kipper tie. New trilby from a good milliners in Halifax. Church's shoes. He looked like a swell from *Guys and Dolls*, but he stood out like a sartorial giant in Brixton's ghetto of post-punk pretension. Mrs Chin was impressed.

'An' when would you be intendin' on movin' in?' she asked.

'As soon as possible, Mrs Chin, depending, of course, on your own commitments.'

She was flattered that a professional, a 'doctor', might be taking up residence.

'An' would it be just you an' the music teacher?' (Nico!)

'Yes . . . very quiet. She may sometimes have a couple of friends round for a glass of amontillado and some Schubert *Lieder*, but apart from that she lives a very frugal and reclusive existence . . . I myself write poetry in the evenings. So, other than the occasional melancholy rattle of the typewriter, there would be very little incursion upon the sensibilities of your other tenants and, of course, your good self.'

'Very nice,' said Mrs Chin, impressed by the good doctor's mixture of dignitas and warm bedside manner. 'Care for some fried plantain?' She offered us a seat at the kitchen table.

'An' what is it you do for a livin'?' she asked me.

I had to fall in with Demetrius's scheme of things. Before I could utter a word he spoke for me.

'James is a medievalist, a diligent scholar reinterpreting the rich legacy of our written history. He spends most of his waking hours researching Carolingian manuscripts in the Bodleian Library – a very painstaking and selfless task, Mrs Chin, I can assure you. Would it be any inconvenience if James were to occasionally prevail upon your hospitality whilst undertaking vital extramural research at the British Museum?'

She looked me in the eye. I could tell she suspected I was a wrong'un. I swallowed my hot slice of plantain and tried, as best I could, to assume the smile of a medievalist.

January '85:

THE REAL THING

Planet Pussy had been invaded by a dreary Garbo movie, and then metamorphosed via Brando's shaven crown from *Apocalypse Now* into a 1½-hour documentary on open-heart surgery. Nico had worked out how to use the video recorder.

Two honest English yeomen, John Cooper Clarke and Echo, were holding target practice in the kitchen. The targets were small black flies on the ceiling, the missiles were jets of blood squirted from hypodermic needles.

The brand new leatherette sofa had already become pockmarked with cigarette burns. Tea had been constantly made, rarely drunk, mostly spilt on the off-white electrostatic nylon carpet. The paper light shade had been torn down and mutilated by Echo, as it reminded him of a 'student gaff'. A naked lightbulb exposed the bare walls. There had been a small mirror, but that had also been removed. There were two armchairs, the brown plastic type covered with cheap foam cushions; your neck stuck to the back whenever you tried to get up. No cooking had ever been done in the kitchen, but the place was filthy. The walls splattered with blood, putrefying takeaway cartons stacked on every available surface. In the fridge was a slow, sad, pink effluent waterfall of melted ice-cream.

There were no proper curtains (Echo was using them as bedding), just nicotine-yellow nets.

The toilet seat had been destroyed (Echo preferred the squatting position as he was prone occasionally to 'a touch of the Michaels'). There had never been any toilet paper.

Demetrius had the back room downstairs as his bedroom. On the floor were heaps of dirty laundry, an overflowing half-abandoned suitcase, bottles of pills, a stack of hardcore porno mags within arm's reach of the bed, and a box of Kleenex . . . scrunched up, semen-cemented tissues were dotted everywhere, like dead carnation-heads.

Upstairs on the right was Nico's room. You entered at your peril. The first thing that hit you was the smell of burnt heroin, hashish, and stale Marlboro smoke – it veiled all other odours, which was probably just as well. Heaps of junk had been deposited everywhere like a fleamarket stall – Nico T-shirts, duty-free bags and empty cigarette cartons, ashtrays piled high beyond overflowing. Nico had a severe catarrh problem, exacerbated by her chainsmoking. (She maintained that she never really started smoking until her habit began – before that she was the singing nun.) By her bed was a Coke tin. The Coke tin had a special function – as a repository for all the phlegm she was continually coughing up. Demetrius had once blindly taken a swig. It's the real thing.

My room was locked. With a chain – until Echo managed to pick his way in. It took him the best part of a weekend. While Nico and I went north to play a gig at the Blackpool Beer Keller to an audience of six (the owner said he didn't care if we went on or not) Echo moved in his entire family, plus pet punk poet pal John Cooper Clarke.

Clarke had just come out of an expensive, intensive, detox clinic – a posh Chelsea sanatorium for addicts of all persuasions, the Charter Clinic. He'd been there to clean himself up at the great expense of his record company. He emerged vulnerable, yet confident, ready to pick up his career. However, Demetrius thought it would be interesting to reintroduce him to Echo. His reasoning was that he felt sorry for Echo being ousted from Nico's employ, he felt somehow personally responsible for him. He thought maybe he could team Echo up with Clarke and together they would make hits – which is exactly what they did. What else are two junkies going to talk about? What else does their whole beleaguered belief system revolve around? Within a couple of hours (as long as it takes to cab from Brixton to Jackie Genova's place in Stoke Newington) they were back on the gear.

Demetrius couldn't bring himself to kick them all out, so a compromise was reached. Faith and the children were put on the first Intercity back to Manchester and Echo and Clarke would sleep in the living-room. Not that it could be actually called sleep, more a kind of stoned somnambulism.

John Cooper Clarke

His own creation. A slim volume. A tall, stick-legged, Rocker Dandy with a bouffant hairdo reminiscent of eighteenth-century Versailles and Dylan circa *Highway 61*. Black biker's jacket with period details, in the top pocket a lace handkerchief, a diamanté crucifix, and a policeman's badge pinned on to the sleeve. He wasn't gay or even camp, his tastes were what you might call School of Graceland. His favourite music was Rock'n'Roll – big guitars, whacking great beat. His favourite eatery was any Little Chef. He particularly enjoyed the cherry pancake with whipped cream – it was consistency of product standard he relished as, without such little oases of sweetness, each day could be an endless series of disappointment, threat and anxiety. He and Echo were almost interchangeable. They both came from the same part of Manchester, they were both Catholics, they were both pure Rock'n'Roll, and they both shared the same needle. The difference being, Clarke had a career.

He performed his poetry in a rapid-fire style taken from the Italian Futurists and a youthful predilection for amphetamine sulphate. His droning Maserati vocal technique sometimes blurred the brilliance of his writing, but everything he did or said had the mark of an individuality born of a true, self-inflicted suffering. Like Echo, he believed in Original Sin. And the Catholic sensibility is capable of nurturing the most original of sins.

He rarely liked to leave the flat, as he had a public persona to maintain. If he did venture out, then he had to prepare the *Grande Levée*. Hair back-combing could take an hour in itself.

Leaving the house was like going on stage. (Echo once delayed his entrance on stage by a whole hour when he commented adversely on Clarke's choice of trousers. Since all his trousers were the same black drainpipes the choice seemed immaterial.) Both of them lived in a world haunted by superstitions and taboos of their own making. Clarke couldn't bear to be near things that weren't manufactured. The 'natural' world was a source of intense dread and disquiet. To tread on grass meant to come into contact with 'the world of worms', a potential holocaust under every cuban-heeled step. He was so like Echo, except his fame had projected him even further out of reality. With commitment and effort he might have become one of our finest People's Poets.

But another poet resided at 23 Effra Road.

Dr Demetrius was taking it all in his ambling stride: gold discs, silver discs, picture discs, black-and-white post-abstract expressionist Soviet constructivist St Martin's College of Art '81 tastefully depressing covers.

Miss Poutnose, the switchboard queen, showed us downstairs, through racks and racks of endless, imperishable product. At last, we were in the Hallowed Halls of Vinyl. To Demetrius it was like a private tour of a bank vault. He'd already planned, before artists and budget had even been discussed, to hit the record company for hundreds of promotional copies which he could use as tour merchandise.

Miss Poutnose brought us a glass of Evian water each. Demetrius's eyes followed her miniskirted behind as it ticktocked enticingly out of reach.

The good doctor finalised an agreeable, though not profligately generous, budget. Master Jonty of the good old family firm Beggars' Banquet was cautious, aware of Nico's unreliability and limited marketability. What, he wanted to know, would be my role? I reassured him of my lowly, yet indispensable status, as arranger. This satisfied him – no one, not even Nico, was to distract John Cale, the producer, from his lofty purpose.

Dids

There was rarely a fixed personnel working with Nico at this time, except for a vague nucleus of myself, Toby, and a manic percussionist from south London called Dids.

Dids had actually emerged on the Manchester scene, banging bits of metal with post-punk art groups. He was a vicious, Puck-like creature, a bit like the kind of thing that used to vomit boiling oil from the towers of medieval cathedrals.

Dids had a haircut that resembled more a piece of topiary than anything one might recognise as a familiar style. It was a cross between convoy hippie and Bauhaus formalism. The sides were shaved completely, while at the back, hanging down his neck, was a raggedy mane. It added further to his elfin appearance. Dids had been brought up in East Grinstead, the south coast holiday resort that houses the H.Q. of the Scientology movement. Dids's dad had been a pal (though not a disciple) of L. Ron Hubbard, the 'Barefaced Messiah' himself. Uncle Ron used to come round for Sunday tea when Dids was a kid. With such a charismatic figure parking his shiny new '61 Thunderbird outside his parents' inauspicious little semi Dids felt an early rapport with showbiz. 'Ow yez. Showtime starts when I leave my front doorstep.' He'd precede every remark with the self-affirmation 'Ow yez', his chest swelling like a bantam cock as he described the unique charms of Balham, his 'manor'. His friends were all car dealers, car repairers and car thieves, and they would give him bits of cars to play with onstage. Anywhere north of the river Thames was suspect to Dids, and as for *Das Kultur*, 'Ow yez. You can really push the mo'or on them or'abahns – nowha'amean?'

We'd done a few things together with Nico. It all sounded a bit like a blind man trying to kick his way out of a scrap yard. What with Toby's thumping great piledriver beat and Dids's clanging old hubcaps, there wasn't much room left for a mere ivory-tickler.

'Ow yez. Industrial groove, mate,' was how Dids described it. Not even Nico's voice could cover that horrendous din of clanging metal. And she had the loudest female voice in Rock'n'Roll.

'John Cale will sort it all out,' said Nico. 'He knows exactly what to do with my music.'

Consistently lazy, Nico still hadn't come up with any new songs, not even a lyric or a line. Demetrius packed her off to a hotel in the Lancashire moors near Pendle Hill (a legendary meeting place for practitioners of the Black Arts). The hotel was located in an area called the Trough of Bowland (it's near the Slough of Despond, close to the Vale of Tears, above the Back of Beyond).

I got a call from Toby.

'It's balderdash, Jim. I'm rock'n'roll, yer know – I've just 'ad an offer from Auto Da Fé – 'eavy metal satanists from Birmingham. One-month residency in Bermuda, then on ter the American circuit . . . more bollox, not the real thing, but I'll be quids in. Got ter do it, sorry, the wife . . . yer know.'

Toby had just got married to a Bruce Springsteen lookalike from Copenhagen. Real tough girl. She could whistle through her teeth and had a knockout punch. Her father was some famous Argentinian primitivist. She was ugly-beautiful, but the ugliness had been in the ascendant, the more smack she used. She and Toby had got themselves fixed up with a nice little habit, as well as a domestic routine. He had to go to Bermuda to get away from himself.

Nico modeling in French *Elle* 1961

Nico, (*third from left*) at age 16 in Fellini's *La Dolce Vita* (Archives Malanga)

Opening Thursday, December 19th
COCKTAIL HOUR
5 to 8 p.m.

The Blue Angel Lounge
featuring the intimate songs of
Nico

All drinks 85¢
152 East 55th Street

No minimum; no cover
PLaza 3-5998

Original invitation to The Blue Angel Lounge, 1964 (Archives Malanga)

A party at The Factory (Fred W. McDarrah)

Nico plays the tambourine in
Velvet Underground publicity
shot (Archives Malanga)

The Velvet Underground: Nico, Sterling Morrison, Maureen Tucker, Lou Reed and John Cale
(Gerard Malanga)

Andy Warhol accompanying Nico, who was the host for a late night horror movie series on a local TV station in Boston. (Archives Malanga)

Paul Morrissey holding Ari, Nico's son by Alain Delon (Fred W. McDarrah)

Nico singing from behind the bar at the Dom, April 11, 1967. (Fred W. McDarrah)

Left, Nico modeling Andy Warhol paper dress stenciled by Gerard Malanga at A&S Department Store in Brooklyn, New York (Fred W. McDarrah)

The Warhol entourage 1968: From left to right, top row: Nico, Brigid Polk, Louis Waldron, Taylor Mead, Ultra Violet, Paul Morrissey, Viva, International Velvet, unidentified person. From left to right, bottom row: Ingrid Superstar, Ondine, Tom Baker, Tiger Morse, Billy Name, Andy Warhol (Archives Malanga)

Nico with The Velvet Underground at the Dom (Fred W. McDarrah)

Publicity shot for *Chelsea Girls* (Billy Name)

Nico sitting next to Taylor Mead at Max's Kansas City (Billy Name)

Nico's *Marble Index* LP cover, 1968 (Guy Webster)

Nico, 1985
(Jill Furmanowsky LFI)

Nico on her final tour (London Features)

COUNTER-INTELLIGENCE

John Cale

John Cale plunged into Dids's miniature elf's lair in Balham. Overweight, overcoat, over here. Hiding his wild coke-stary eyes beneath scratched Wayfarers, covering his beer-barrel gut with a stained sweatshirt and a No-Smoking sticker. This was the man who'd directed the aesthetic of New York's most stylish pop-group. Distanced now, by more than a decade, from the marketing genius of Warhol and the savvy of Reed, he'd had to take on the narcotic, alcoholic and psychic abuse alone. Yet beneath the overcoat, the distended belly and the bloated ego you sensed there might still exist a good-looking, almost likeable, Welsh grammar-school boy on the make.

Dids's living-room was suddenly full of him. He commandeered the coffee-table, emptied a wrap of coke, and carved out four massive lines – one for me, one for Dids and two for himself. I don't think we'd even said 'Hello'.

He pulled a videocassette from out of his overcoat pocket. It was one of those clanging competitions between me, Dids, Toby and poor Nico. After less than a minute he pressed Stop:

'What's *this* called?' he asked in his West Village/Welsh Village accent. 'Strangers on a Stage?'

It was Godawful. Nico fighting to be heard. The rest of us ignoring her completely – showing off our skills, selling our wares, like barrow-boys on Balham market. No one, at any time, had stopped to listen.

'Where's the drummer?' he asked.

'Ow yez . . . Old Tobe . . . Doin' a stretch on the Pina Colada circuit dahn in Bermew-da,' said Dids, pleased to have the drum stool to himself.

'That's a pity,' said Cale. 'He's the only one who plays in time.'

Dids was deeply offended. He was about to spit some Balham bile at this Son of the Valleys, but he bit his tongue instead, remembering who held the job-cards.

Back in Brixton, Demetrius had given over his room to Cale for the duration. (Cale being too tight to rent a place of his own.) Cale took one look at John Cooper Clarke and Echo:

'Get the fuck out!' He pointed to the open door.

It was 4.00 a.m. TV transmission had stopped and there was just a fizz of white noise – neither of them had bothered to turn it off.

Clarke was standing in the middle of the room, bent double, seemingly comatose.

I switched off the red-hot set.

'I wuz watchin' that,' said Clarke.

He was, too. He'd probably made the attempt to turn off the TV at close-down, a couple of hours before, but had abandoned such a Herculean task and was locked in a neo-paralysis half-way across the living-room floor. Echo, meanwhile, had been playing with the aimer, creating patterns out of the seemingly random white dots. Shoals of electric anchovies were swimming across the screen.

'I thought I just told you to *get out*!' Cale repeated.

'Who the fook's this obnoxious swine?' Echo asked me, ignoring the irate Welshman, resting his head on a pillow in motionless indifference.

'John Cale,' answered John Cale.

'Oh . . .' said Clarke, still bent double. 'One of our Welsh cousins . . . not renowned for their politesse.'

'Where did you get that pillow?' Cale snapped at Echo, snatching it from behind his head. 'You got it from my room, didn't you, eh, didn't you?' He marched off to Demetrius's bedroom, pillow tucked under his arm, and slammed the door.

Clarke and Echo left the next day. The ambience shifted abruptly from smack to booze. Beer crates were stacked in the kitchen, six-packs chilling in the once-empty fridge, bottles of vodka abandoned where they dropped.

Over the following few days, Cale rambled a broken mono-logue, referring to things he may or may not have mentioned previously. Blurred by booze, confused by coke, it was hard to follow the sudden leaps of association. I got caught in his mad Welsh rhapsody. He loved to talk plots and intrigues. Paranoid conspiracy theories were his brain-food. I'd be on the edge of sleep, when there'd be a knock at my door:

'James! Wake up! Listen! It says here that terrorist groups in Europe are being covertly funded by powerful economic inter-ests in the U.S., in order to prolong European disunity and subordination to the power of the dollar. Whatd'youthinkof thatthen, eh?' He'd wait for an answer. A paranoid insomniac with a bottle of Stolichnaya in one hand and a wrap of coke in the other. He tried to blanket his high-toned Welshness under that heavy Manhattan overcoat, but those ringing, singing vowels gave him away – like a rotting sheep or a male voice choir, there was no mistaking their origins.

Cale was clearly nuts, but it made a change to be working with someone who had energy and who was both gifted and dedicated to his profession. Nico had an inherent talent – her voice, her persona – but she was lazy and morose. Cale, on the other hand, possessed a skill that he'd worked at and a set of creative principles that he'd tested and honed down rigorously into one simple aesthetic credo: 'Keep it simple'.

Demetrius brought his Bullworker and Nico back from the Trough of Bowland.

'So, Johnny Viola.' Nico hadn't seen Cale in a couple of years. 'Put on a little weight, I see.' This seemed to delight her, other people letting themselves go.

At last Nico had some songs, in varying stages of

completion. Some had the melody but not the words, others vice versa. We listened to a couple she'd recorded on her cassette player. Rough as they were, they sounded a thousand times more focused than the clanging competitions we'd done on the video nasty. Even in her indolence Nico had an essential style that was uniquely her own. It worked – with that damned harmonium. Anything we might add was a superficial distraction, artifice. We were merely gatecrashers on her talent.

The Strongroom had just been completed. A state-of-the-art, top-of-the-middle-range studio, located in a converted warehouse in Shoreditch. We got it cheap because we were the first. Everything looked good – but what exactly was I looking at? Little red dots that winked intriguingly in the blackness. A huge mixing console. Instant studio-to-desk monitoring. Stacks of gadgets and FX. Diffused lighting. Ambient colour scheme. Everything to seduce you away from what you should be doing.

'Keep it simple' would be a tough aesthetic to follow in such tempting surroundings.

Demetrius ferried Nico to the studio. She'd been to see some Harley Street shrink earlier, who told her that Demetrius was an 'enabler', someone whose emotional dependency on her facilitated her dependency on heroin. This interpretation of need had increased Nico's paranoia. She was clutching her lyric sheet as if it was an audition.

Recording studios are a place where you try to preserve the memory of a musical experience you had somewhere else. For a performer like Nico they were discomforting. She needed a live atmosphere, a sense of place, to do her stuff – not a laboratory, however tasteful the decor. With a live audience at least you can project yourself at something. In a studio your audience is potentially that much greater, but invisible.

Maybe a shot would help.

The control room and the acoustic room were separated by two glass doors six feet apart. They formed a kind of booth. On one side was Cale, myself and Dave Young the engineer (Dids was outside somewhere poking about the alleyways and construction sites, looking for bits of scrap metal he could utilise for his artistic purpose). On the other side was a large acoustic room that housed a grand piano and looked out on to the London sky. In between sat Nico, hermetically sealed between the two glass doors, like a slide specimen.

Dave miked up the harmonium. This took some time. With a non-electric, unpluggable instrument, you have to work out exactly where to position the microphones. Dave was both a serious player as well as a button-presser, but the harmonium proved something of a problem. ('Like a dinosaur with bad breath,' commented Cale.) It seemed to have developed an arthritic creak in its pedals and a strange, high-pitched squeak, like a rusty wheelchair. Dave got rid of the creak, but the squeak remained, more pronounced than ever.

Cale switched off all the studio lights. Now it was just darkness, Nico's voice, and the little red dots.

> They will give you what you need
> They will run your life.
> They will get you where they want you
> On the cross you'll die.
> What a game,
> Our fair frame,
> Consumed into a single flame.

Demetrius had embedded himself in the warm labial folds of a soft black leather sofa. He hugged his Bullworker, squeezing it tightly between his thighs. As Nico's song rose to its climax he pushed down on the tensely sprung steel – *uuhnnn* – and collapsed on the floor, nose to nose with Cale's fungoid trainers.

Cale was on his spy riff again: 'So, your father could speak six languages, including Russian and Turkish, eh? Used to travel to Eastern Europe all the time? What was he up to, we all ask ourselves?'

'I don't know what you mean, Jaaawn,' said Nico, defensively.

'Counter-intelligence,' – Cale's Welsh accent stressed the

first syllable of every sentence – 'Espionage . . . it's the only logical explanation for someone of his background and education . . . what else could he do?'

'He didn't like to do anything much, he was lazy, like me.' She winked at me knowingly.

'Exactly . . . posh family, overeducated, indolent – ideal secret service material.'

'Oh really, John, you're getting tooo much.'

'Not at all. James, don't you agree? You know – Oxford and all that.'

'Well, John, you're thinking of Cambridge,' I said. 'Oxford's got the dreaming spires, it's Cambridge that's got the spying dreamers.'

'Whatever. The point is, it stands to reason – Nico's father was involved in counter-intelligence. Probably even a double agent, considering early Soviet policy towards the Hitler régime.'

Spies were everywhere. Cale's pathological suspicions of clandestine agents lurking in our midst ensured that we had a twenty-four-hour lockout. No one unconnected with Nico's album would be allowed to enter the studio. Unless, of course, it was the delivery boy from the pub, bringing the evening's crates of Grolsch.

Nico worked through the only songs she had over the following few days. Just the six, with harmonium accompaniment. It wasn't a lot to go on. Certainly not enough to satisfy the record company, or the purchaser. She suggested we do 'My Funny Valentine' and an old German ballad called 'Das Lied von Der einsamen Mädchen' ('The Song of the Lonely Girl' – all blood-red lips and death-white skin, juvenilia). No one rushed to greet her suggestions.

Cale was aware of the limited studio time available, we didn't have an extendable budget. Where big-time pop stars might spend a year polishing up the right triangle sound, we had three weeks to get the whole thing written, arranged, produced and recorded, ready for the test pressing. Cale suggested Nico should leave us to it and come back towards the end to

re-do her vocals. In the meantime, the rest of us would disman-
tle and rebuild the songs around the guide vocals she'd put
down.

Nico's songs were like mini-dramas – they depended upon
pauses and silence. There was no inherent rhythm that suggested itself, and no sense in which she kept strict time, as there
was no intrinsic pulse. Thus, a rhythm track would have to be
created against a vocal line that wavered and faltered. A drummer's nightmare.

Dids arrived at the studio the next day, expecting Nico to be
there, ready to work on the rhythm tracks with her, getting
everything just tight. He was aghast at the task that had been
left to him, trying to play around a nervous, stoned Nico
singing songs she only half knew. He stormed across the acoustic room to set up his drum kit. Standing tense and erect against
Nico's harmonium was a Bullworker. Dids's head jerked to one
side, he peered at the alien intruder from the corner of his eye
like an enraged rooster, and threw the offending object across
the room. It bounced off the wall, leaving a thin crack veining
across the pristine colour scheme.

Wherever you sat an empty bottle would alert you to Cale's
presence. He turned the studio upside-down, making it his own.
And then he turned myself and Dids upside-down for ideas.
Administering profligate quantities of drugs and booze, 'keep
it simple' became a fractured legend. One musical idea or
phrase would become instantly superseded by another and
yet another until they were all subsumed beneath a 3.00 a.m.
alcoholic blur.

'Now, *doant* discuss anything of what goes on in here.' (The
spies.) 'Pass a beer! There's a squeak on the bass drum pedal . . .'
(Swigs beer. Farts.) 'Gimme that blade.' (Chop. Chop. Chop.)
Got a note?' (sniffs) '. . . HMNYEEAH . . .' (pockets note).

The delivery boy would arrive with beer and champagne.
Coke dealers would slither in and out. Cale's manager, Dan
Saliva, would come in, a supercilious sneer on his face, jangling
his keys, wincing at the teutonic cacophony, suggesting we do a
Jim Morrison song.

'Think of America, John, think of America.'

Each song was virgin territory. Dids was tearing himself apart on a song called 'Tananore', trying to follow Nico's vocal without wandering massively out of time. Cale suggested a flat, trotting rhythm that would cover any snags, a sound like the banging of a coffin lid. He found an old suitcase used to house Dids's car parts, placed it across his knees like a set of bongos, and miked it up. We had the basis of a rhythm track.

Other songs he'd ask me to play blind, without thinking about keys or chord changes. He'd record layers of ideas, colours and textures, to play with later on at the mixing stage. We had endless arguments about this. He'd switch off all the studio lights so I couldn't even see my keyboard.

Sleep cost money. It meant the studio wasn't being used. We were all in that semi-trance state that the mind gets into when regular sleep-patterns are broken. Cale would stagger off into the night, looking for some action, banging on the doors of some low-rent bacchanal, demanding to be admitted. Instead of rugby, he'd found art, but he still wandered the streets at midnight, like a boozed-up boyo.

Nico returned, suggesting we do the two cover songs – not that she was wildly keen about them herself, she just couldn't come up with any more original material, and we were running out of time. We put them down. She sang 'Valentine' well, like a graveside elegy, but it still seemed out of place, a cabaret spotlight on a cream grand piano in a Gothic ruin.

We still had to make up one more track. I had an idea to put down something that would somehow encapsulate the whole Brixton/Nico/Cale experience. A kind of musical distillation of the fragmentary video we were subjected to back at Effra Road. I played a keyboard melody and suggested Cale recite a passage from *Tropic of Capricorn*: 'The last white man pulling the trigger on the last emotion . . .' To which we added blasts of Nico's Lorelei foghorn. Then, finally, Dids came downstairs from the studio kitchen carrying an assortment of pots, pans and kettles. He arranged them on the floor in a circle and sat in the middle, playing his bric-à-brac Balham gamelan. Way down upon the Mekong Delta with Crazy Christa and Psycho Johnny.

Back in Brixton Cale couldn't/wouldn't sleep. He'd blunder around the flat all night long, playing endless mixes on a ghetto-blaster. Nico gave him a shot to knock him out, he was bugging us so badly. He spent the next day puking up the consequences. The alleyway up to the studio was an archipelago of vomit atolls.

At the end of three weeks we just had to leave it and walk away. There were some good ideas and one really standout track, called 'König'. A beautiful, almost chorale-like piece. Cale wanted to do an arrangement for it, but I urged him to leave it alone. Just Nico and the harmonium, her voice cracking at times, yet free – unencumbered by anyone else's image of her. No need to give her a setting, or dress her up in modernity. What she had was her own.

'König'
Oh König lass Dich leiten
Lass mich Dich begleiten
Oh König lass Dich leiten
Lass mich Dich begleiten

Auf diesem weiten Strand
Ergreife meine Hand.

Ich will Dir alles geben
Dass Dich am Leben hält
Ein Hoffen und ein Streben
Dein Blick ist in mein Zelt.

'King'
(Oh King let yourself be led
Let me escort you
Oh King let yourself be led
Let me escort you.

On this wide shore
Take hold of my hand

I want to give you everything
That will keep you alive

Hope and Striving
Your glance falls into my tent.)

As I put my key into the lock I heard a noise to my left. I looked down. Hiding behind one of the stone lions was Echo.

'Echo, is that you? . . . What are you doing?'

'Doin'? Doin'? A'm gonna do 'im, that's what! The boyo – the sheepshagger.' He stepped dramatically out of the shadows, thumping his fist into his hand. He had a thick brass knuckleduster.

'Jesus, Echo . . .' I'd never seen a knuckleduster before. It weighed down my hand. You could break someone's jaw with one blow. Two would kill. I let him in, told him to put the weapon away and made him a bed on the sofa.

Cale had gone. Nico was in her room listening to her new album over and over again.

'There's somethin' about that moon I don't like,' said Echo, 'now yer see it, now yer don't – day in, day out. I'm fookin' sick, Jimmy.' He left me his sketch book to peruse, the one marked PRIVATE, while he went upstairs to knock on Nico's door.

The first page had a picture of John Cooper Clarke on the cross. Instead of INRI it bore the inscription I ♥ NEW YORK. Another had Nico in a parody of a renaissance Madonna and child, crouched in her black cloak, as if nursing the infant Jesus. When you looked closer you could see her strapped up and tourniqué'd, ready to hit the vein. I turned the pages: me, playing a grand piano whose curves metamorphosed into a recumbent naked Venus. Demetrius as a bright pink devil with the fires of hell glowing on his naked skin . . . in his right hand, instead of a pitchfork, a Bullworker; in his left a swagbag with dollar bills falling out, his beard trimmed wickedly, and two little nascent horns protruding from his bald pate. Like a medieval bestiary the book contained the phantasmagoria of Echo's everyday existence.

THE SONS OF SLUMBER

As soon as Cale had left, Echo and John Cooper Clarke were reinstalled. Clarke had been doing some shows promoted by Demetrius. Echo was always there, the emperor's food-taster, personal valet, 'Wife even,' said Nico. Clarke would always bring home the necessaries, like a good husband. The two of them would spend entire evenings taking shot after shot until they were dangerously close to OD:

'Amma goin', John, amma?'

'Aye . . . yer turnin' blue. . .'

'Amma, John . . . amma?'

They'd take turns to see who dared touch the chill hand of Papa Death.

Nico was caught up in pre-release publicity platitudes. Interminable interviews with the same old soundtrack: '. . . Aaaandy . . . Looooou . . . Jaaawn . . . Aaaandy . . . Veeelvet . . . Loooou . . . Aaandy . . .'

She still hadn't come up with a title for the album.

'How about: Morphia and the Sons of Slumber?' I'd suggested. She gave me her stun-gun look and tapped the hypodermic, deadening any air-bubbles.

Demetrius suggested her backing group should find a name, that way our jobs would be safeguarded. Bookers would want the whole package. I was stuck on 'the Sons of Slumber', but Nico just wouldn't have it. In fact she didn't want anyone else's name anywhere on the album cover.

'OK then – what about NICO very big and the Sons of

Slumber, very small?' I appealed to her. 'It has a definite ring to it, don't you think?'

'Jim . . . you are reedeeeculous, always joking. That English sense of humooor . . . you know I don't get it.'

'But I'm *serious*,' I protested.

She tutted, and loaded the open-heart surgery video into the player. Clarke and Echo perked up – there was a particular sequence they liked, a configuration of clamps and catheters, peeled flesh and subcutaneous fat, all of this intercut with snippets of the tape's previous occupant, Kurtz/Brando: 'The Horror . . . the Horror . . .'

'Come on, Nico – tell us a joke,' I suggested, wearying of the collage of bloodstained scalpels and crumbling pagodas.

'But I don't know any jokes.'

'You must know *one*,' I persisted.

'No, really, I don't . . .'

Clarke was amazed. 'Everybody should know *one* joke, Nico.'

'Yeh,' said Echo, 'yer never know 'oo yer might get banged up with.'

'Banged up?' she was puzzled. 'You mean like sharing a needle?'

'No . . . *Banged up*, pleasurin' 'er Majesty . . .'

'Oooo, I see.' She smiled and nodded understanding. 'You mean, *in the bedroooom*.'

'He means in *jail*, Nico,' I said, killing the confusion.

'Oooh . . . yeees . . .' She pondered the impossible mysteries of the English language. Clarke remained incredulous: 'Straight up – yer don't know *one* joke?'

'Honestly, John, I've told you. We Germans have no sense of huuumooor.'

'Yer right,' said Echo. 'If they 'ad, they'd 'ave copped the resemblance ter Charlie Chaplin.'

Again, Nico was lost. Echo rarely introduced the subject-matter of his observations.

Clarke was still intrigued by Nico's jokeless personality: 'I know . . . why don't yer just try ter learn *one* joke? Think of all the new friends yer could make . . . yer need a sense of 'umour, yer can't get through this world on charm alone, Nico.'

'I just don't seem to remember them.'

'*Try*,' said Clarke. He launched into his repertoire. It was a private performance even funnier than his public ones. All the vicious, really funny jokes the Alternative crowd disapprove of.

We'd wait after each one . . . waiting, not necessarily for laughter, but for some click of understanding. It never came. She just didn't get it. We went back to the open-heart video.

Clarke squeezed a subtle hint of lemon juice into his elixir of happiness and heated the base of the spoon with his lighter: 'I've been readin' about this completely new type of birth pill . . .' He pulled back the dropper and filled the empty syringe. 'Yer swallow one an' it's like yer were never born.' He handed the hypodermic to Echo, who had his vein up and ready. As Echo injected his share, Clarke tightened a polka-dot tie round his forearm, bracing himself for Echo's administration of the remaining half-shot. Clarke still feared yet loved the needle, a novice at communion.

Nico began to shake, silently and slowly, then her shoulders began to jig up and down: 'H'mmmm . . . Ho Ho . . .'

Clarke and Echo closed their eyes in mutual prayer, sensing the benign radiance of Mother Love as she poured divine unction into their abject souls. Without committing mortal sin, smacking up was the only way two males could come together.

'. . . H'mmmm . . . Ho Ho . . . H'mmmm . . . Ho Ho . . . Like you were never boooorn . . . Ho Ho Ho Ho Ho Ho . . .'

Nico came up with a title for the album: *Camera Obscura*. Demetrius and I smuggled a name for the group on to the cover. 'Something small,' he'd suggested. Clarke and Echo came up with *The Faction*. Nondescript, diminutive. That's how Nico liked us.

When she saw the sleeve she freaked.

'Who's this fucking Faction?' She made it sound like Fucktion.

Everyone shrugged. 'It's you, Jim, isn't it?'

'OK, it's me.'

'You've got a damned cheek – on *my* album.'

'If you're so concerned about *your* album, how come you were only present in the studio for four days out of the three weeks?'

I just wanted to chisel a little foothold somewhere – she wouldn't give an inch. I knew she'd be straight on the phone to Demetrius.

'That Jim, so puuushy. Who does he think he is, huh? Can't we get someone else?'

The album came out to kind reviews. The serious doom-dwellers went into ecstasies. Mostly critics just seemed to be reassured by the fact that Nico was still alive somewhere, so long as it wasn't in their vicinity.

Beggar's Banquet went for the safe option and released 'My Funny Valentine' as the single. The more I heard it, the more I hated it. It wasn't Nico's fault especially in choosing the song, or mine for its bland piano and unnecessary trumpet arrangement. There had been so little time to do anything interesting with it, to reinvent it, make it say something. I dreamed of a steady, funereal, E-flat figure on the piano, repeated throughout the piece, and held together by simple architectural chords, like a Delphic tomb. Instead it sounded like a drag act in a half-dead cabaret. But then, maybe that's what everyone wanted.

SUSPICIOUS MINDS

It was two thousand years since the last Poetry Olympics flop at the Albert Hall . . . people would have forgotten. Time for another bout of logorrhoea. The Beatniks' revenge.

John Cooper Clarke had been slipped on the bill as a young(ish) contender so Demetrius finally got the chance to get to Allen Ginsberg, the headline act. Nico knew Ginsberg from the good old days back at the Dom – in fact she'd borrowed the harmonium idea from him. Demetrius and Ginsberg had a shared enthusiasm . . . Enthusiasm. Demetrius championed Ginsberg because he was never really 'hip', being too much of a celebrant . . . the nebbish at the centre of every groovy scene, holding a candle, chanting his homoerotic mantras. He'd get excited and take off his clothes in the presence of people who were too cool to remove their RayBans. He was Dr Demetrius's kind of guy.

Demetrius quickly elected himself as Ginsberg's road manager and fixed him up with a rentagig reading in Liverpool. Nico and I tagged along.

Ginsberg was dressed in a check jacket, white shirt and tie, his beard neatly trimmed. He looked like an elderly Emeritus professor of American literature, rather than the guru of mutual masturbation. Demetrius seemed a bit disappointed. As the exhausted Citroën panted up the M6, the conversation limped along behind.

'How smaaart you look now, Allen,' remarked Nico.

'Weell you know, times have changed. I'm told the Buddah

would wear a jacket and tie now, and host his own talk show, on cable of course.'

'Well, I'm not so sure about that, Allen,' said Demetrius, offended by the image.

'Neither am I,' he chuckled.

Rather than the hoped-for instant bridge of sensibilities between the two men of letters, Demetrius encountered an immediate chasm of understanding, constantly widened by their attempts at conversation. Demetrius had believed that Ginsberg was the true inheritor of the Whitman flame, the Ecstatic Priapic, an unrepentant self-pleasurer.

But . . . the Master Beat, it turned out, was not a true man of the people. He didn't endorse the simple and honest virtues of the people's music (Country & Western). Nor did he honour the memory of the people's sovereign. The King:

> We're caught in a trap
> I can't walk out
> Because I love you too much, Baby.

'I really can't,' said Ginsberg, the words muffled by a mouthful of cheese and onion crisps, 'see any redeeming qualities in the music of Elvis Presley. I'm sorry . . .' He really did seem sorry.

Demetrius turned up the cassette. 'Just listen to this, Allen.' He sang along in that bluff, hunker-down baritone:

> We can't go on together
> With suspicious minds
> And we can't build our dreams
> On suspicious minds.

'There you go, Allen,' Demetrius paused the cassette. '*We can't build our dreams on suspicious minds*. What a line!'

Ginsberg shook his head. 'Once again, I'm sorry, I just don't see it.' To him it was just honky music, whiter than a Klansman's hood. 'Compared with an artist of Dylan's depth and originality, Presley is pure Vegas Schlock.'

'Bloody 'ell, Allen, you're talking about the King there.' Demetrius was wounded. He canvassed Nico's opinion.

Nico was smoking a thin, single joint like a rollup, of opiated hash. She mulled over the message of the dead King, then smiled at everyone. 'You know, there's this new birth pill, that when you take it, it's like you were never boorn . . . funny, huh?' She laughed.

Ginsberg popped open another bag of crisps and offered them round. It kept our mouths wordlessly occupied.

Demetrius had hoped he might be in for some *On the Road* epiphanies. Ginsberg, perhaps, hoped he might be in for some Front-Line Brixton Faggotry. (I'd expressed interest in his small Indian pump-organ. I think he got the wrong idea.)

Nico just seemed happy to be with someone older than herself, who endorsed some of the same Dionysiac myths. For Artist Guru, read Favourite Uncle.

Ginsberg seemed genuinely to go for the good in people, straight away. Demetrius's competitiveness and cock-size comparisons were of little interest to him. There was a seriousness behind the hedonism and an austerity beneath the hyperbole. He was a kindly man who held strong beliefs, the belief in happiness being paramount. He just didn't like Elvis Presley.

We weren't accustomed to such positivism and the dank European fog of pessimism took a little time to lift . . . though, strangely, not from Nico's shoulders. She seemed almost childlike with him, less tortured. Enriched by his spiritual largesse.

Demetrius's father, Big Lionel, was a gruff, bluff, Manchester patriarch. The Tyrannosaurus Rex of the Rotary Club. He detested all lesser reptiles like his son's associates and thought Demetrius Jr an unworthy recipient of the family chemist fortune. He'd had three heart attacks already – one for each of his sons.

Demetrius Jr had witnessed Ginsberg's dignified professorial manner at the Albert Hall. Perhaps a poetry recital would reassure his father that his son was at last engaged in serious cultural pursuits.

The dressing-room was unlike any I'd ever seen. People talking quietly, holding glasses of white wine at shoulder level.

Women in frocks, men in suits, cheese on sticks, a couple of bearded Robin Hall and Jimmie McGregor lookalikes discussing ballad form by the beer tray. There was no one puking, fighting, shooting up, or sulking.

Nico wandered around the chattering forest of literary wind, a lost child smoking an opium joint.

I remained, the corner paranoiac, aware only of a slight whiff of body odour, of nervous provincialism, of defeat. Allen was the most famous poet in the world. Not as famous as a medium-level pop-star would be, but it was an extraordinary achievement, nonetheless. You could detect little bite-size morsels of envy, they popped in and out of mouths, like the skewered cubes of sweating cheddar: 'This psychedelic Rabbi, this media-manipulator, this Half-Holy Fool of the Beautiful People gets everywhere, all the time. How does the bastard find time to write? Huh, no wife, no kids of course . . . Gay, you know . . . the first to come out, they say . . . Quite courageous really, in the middle of McCarthyism . . . H'mmmm, he has been around rather a long time, though . . .'

The cheese-and-winos left the dressing-room and took their seats in the hall. Big Lionel was escorted to the 'Reserved' row.

Nico offered Ginsberg some of her joint (a rare act) before he went on stage. He paused, then as if resolving against false resolutions, accepted it, sipping little by little the tarry euphoria. He passed it to Demetrius, who shook his head.

'No, no, Allen, never, not for me . . . the mirror is already distorted.'

'Are you going to take your clothes off, Allen?' Nico asked.

In front of the 'mild, withdrawn English', we'd have to see.

Nico and I took our places at the back, directly behind Big Lionel and Demetrius.

Ginsberg began by chanting the Padma Sambhava mantra: 'Om Ah Hum . . .' seated on a chair, squeeze-box on his knees, sustaining a single-note drone. The embarrassment prickled, but it was bearable. People half expected the chanting. What made the audience crave invisibility, though, was Ginsberg's increasingly homosexual subject-matter.

He lubricated our sensibilities with 'Red cheeked boyfriends tenderly kiss me sweet-mouthed/Under Boulder coverlets winter springtime . . .' Gently he slipped in the 'happy hard-ons'.

Then he yelled a climactic sonnet to the stretched sphincter: 'Fuck me in the ass! Suck me! Come in my ears!/I want those pink Abdominal Bellybuttons!'

The veins in Big Lionel's neck bulged. His skin turned red to purple with barely suppressed outrage.

After the reading Big Lionel refused to shake the hand of the sodomite, the fellator of blond boys, the man who washed his

After the reading Big Lionel refused to shake the hand of the sodomite, the fellator of blond boys, the man who washed his own arse like a street Arab. Instead he exploded at Demetrius: 'My Godfathers! Call that poetry? That I should desert my hearth and home to be subjected to the foul-mouthed ravings of a bearded nancy.'

In the dressing-room the serious Liverpool literati gathered as Ginsberg carefully packed his squeeze-box. Mersey Beat Poets. Beards and BeBop glasses. Thelonius Monk and the Man in the Moon.

Nico poured herself a glass of warm Liebfraumilch and shook her head; she seemed disappointed.

'What's up?' I asked.

'I thought Allen *always* took his clothes off,' she sighed.

BLOP

The music of *Camera Obscura* was complicated and illogical. Structures were there, but they weren't easy to remember: they mostly defied the remorseless logic of the traditional pop song, i.e. intro, verse, chorus, verse, chorus, middle eight, brief jazzy squirt of wine-bar saxophone, verse, chorus, fade to sax and repeated hook – sax player collects cheque. The songs had been only half written to begin with, then recomposed in the studio, assembled, like a collage, but without the use of pre-existing material. Every musical detail had been engendered spontaneously under studio conditions and although alcohol and drugs are a cheap form of inspiration (at merely financial rather than spiritual cost) I felt chances had been taken. Rock 'musicians' often forget they're in the Image Industry and get cosmic delusions of grandeur, imagining they're in the same lineage as Beethoven and Mozart. For all her doom-laden seriousness, Nico spared us any nauseating prattle about her 'art'. And all we were doing was just ganging up around her name. It was only a little thing. Just enough to get us out and about.

Occasionally she would hint at a more exacting creative purpose. She wished she'd made a success of acting – but, she was the first to admit, it required a diligence and an intellectual discipline she didn't possess. It wasn't exactly a regret, she'd made her choice and allowed Warhol to add his signature to her persona, but, back then with Fellini, 'if only I'd got up on time!'

The sporadic bursts of fame or notoriety would, in the meantime, sustain her in the knowledge that, unable to get out

of bed, she'd done what she could. Essentially, she loved to do
nothing more than lie in her room, smoking and listening to a
Mahler concert on her tinny radio, hypodermic reassuringly
within arm's reach. It was a life measured out in Marlboro butts.

We previewed the album at Ronnie Scott's. As we'd only just
left the recording studio it was a tense occasion, no one knew
the material that well. This meant that we underplayed and, I
think, considering the kitchen-sink nature of previous concerts,
our inhibitions worked to the music's advantage.

The real showcase for Nico's new progeny, its relaunch into
the artocracy, occurred at Chelsea Town Hall. It was an
inspired setting, chosen by Demetrius. Just a short walk from
the Charter Clinic and thus within easy access of the celebrity
junkies. It was an occasion whose significance would inevitably
reverberate throughout the drug community. Lots of 'lovies'
and 'darlings' and 'poor Georgina had a terrible fix this afternoon and puked all over the kilim'.

Demetrius had been persisting in his courtship of the Beat
Literati and had forged an attachment to Carolyn Cassady, the
wife of Neal (who, as Dean Moriarty, was the hero of
Kerouac's *On the Road*). Although she was twenty years
Demetrius's senior, she had a young female companion with
her who might provide the ideal literary (and erotic) muse for
his poetic soul.

The debts had been mounting. Not counting the whole U.S.
tour, I still hadn't been paid for a whole succession of shows,
plus there was a percentage share due on the advance for Nico's
album. Demetrius and I came to an agreement that there would
be a settling of accounts at the Chelsea show.

Nico gave her best performance yet and at last her accompaniment sounded convincing. Her authority on stage was
absolute and the gig proved to be a landmark that reaffirmed
her legend and, for the druggists, vindicated a whole way of life
. . . you could be a really bad girl and still get away with it. I no
longer felt ashamed or embarrassed for her or myself. The
music was an integrated whole – it managed to be a summation
of her past and a direction for the future.

The past was the hardest aspect of her repertoire to deal with – those Velvet Underground songs that people, naturally, expected to hear. How to revitalise them? Nico had become so utterly bored with them, locking into automatic pilot whenever they came up in the set. I suggested she sang 'All Tomorrow's Parties' a cappella. No other accompaniment could better John Cale's arrangement – that nagging ostinato octave D on the piano with the relentless death-march tumbril-tread of the drums. Stripped of its 'blackened shroud' and 'hand-me-down gown' the naked voice resounded about the hall, underlining the hollowness of the subject matter. For 'Femme Fatale' we did a kind of Sugarplum Fairy parody with a toy piano. For the first time in a while the tart humour came out from behind those lyrics and the rather earnest art-house solemnity that surrounded the Velvet Underground was briefly dispelled.

After the encores (!) I asked Demetrius if we could settle up. He called me a capitalist. What should have been an occasion for celebration and congratulation turned instead into another pathetic and ugly farce with me diving off the stage on top of Demetrius, even as the audience were leaving and Carolyn Cassady and the future Demetrieuse were lining themselves up for an evening's Beat-itudes and impromptu free verse.

We made up later, but by then it was too late. The aesthetes were aghast at such rough-house vulgarity and Demetrius's love-life was forced to take yet another strange twist:

The Couchette of Dr Demetrius

(In the Erotes, written by Lucian in the second century A.D., we are told of how a youth, enamoured by the beauty of Praxiteles's statue of Aphrodite, contrived to hide himself one night in the temple of the goddess of love, at Knidos. A flaw in the marble of one of Aphrodite's thighs was interpreted as a semen stain, evidence of the intensity of the youth's ardour.)

On the top bunk of an Intercity couchette Omega, the Moon Goddess, sleeps soundly. The dull opiate fallen from her hand, she sails her barque of dreams down the winding River Styx to rest her weary head on Hades's darkest shore.

Upon the other bank her suitor stands – one Demetrius, erstwhile physician to Dionysus himself, the great God of Mischief and Merriment, Appetite and Lust. In leaner years the medicant has been a mere spectator at the feast, looking on with educated disdain as the ignorant and carefree revellers indulge their reckless appetites. Now, cast out for quackery and knavishness from the benign patronage of the Great Gods' Court, he has vowed to return as Demetrius the Enabler, vanquish those who mock his genius, and claim for his own the hand of the fair Omega, daughter of Morpheus, the God of Sleep.

By his side the Sword of Theseus, the Bullworker; in his hand the Chalice of Valium, the Confidence Builder; he braves the swelling tide of the libidinous waves to stand, at last, upon the pagan shore and bestow his silver testament, the seed of his longing, upon the sleeping form of the beloved Omega.

'Naturally, I wiped it off afterwards. Wouldn't wish to leave a stain on her character.'

The Connoisseurs

J. C-CLARKE [*quizzically*]: I don't know if I don't prefer the brown stuff or the white. [*Measures a double dose*]
ECHO: Generally speakin' as a regular tipple, I'm more in favour of the brown . . . it's warmer some'ow.
J. C-CLARKE: I know, there's more of a softer glow about the Eye-ranian stuff, it lingers that much longer . . . with the China white, on the other 'and, it's 'arder – I must say I sometimes feel chastened by its astringency.
[*Phone rings. Echo picks up receiver, then replaces it.*]
ECHO: Plus, the brown stuff is that much more dependable . . . I've rarely bin disappointed. . .
J. C-CLARKE: Whereas the white can be bleached ter fuck.
[*Echo presses J. C-Clarke's arm to find a vein. Slips needle in gently, at horizontal angle. Then administers himself a shot.*]
J. C-CLARKE [*leaning against kitchen wall, head slumped*]: . . . The brown . . . [*ten-second pause*] . . . or the white?

[They both stare at the floor.]
ECHO: . . . I must say though . . .
J. C-CLARKE and ECHO in unison: I could just do with some of
the white right now. *[Fade]*

The Effra Road flat directly overlooked the Fridge. Beggar's
Banquet had commissioned a Nico video, and the director and
crew (a couple of trainee directors who'd never even heard of
Nico) thought the Fridge would be an ideal location for their
big break. The Fridge had been an unprofitable theatre until it
had been gutted by fire. Now that it was a burnt-out ruin,
stinking of charred wood, soot and ash, it had become a
favoured nightspot for the Brixton crowd. Nico had to mime
and lip-synch the vocals for a breezy little number called 'My
Heart Is Empty'. Try as she might, she could barely remember
the words, let alone mouth them.

The director was obsessed by my watch.

'It's all about the concept of Entropy . . . the erosion of
beauty . . . the inexorable march of time.' He'd point his stupid
camera at my wristwatch, then pan across to Nico's face. In the
end she just kept opening and closing her mouth, more, it
seemed, in an effort to breathe (the soot and the dust) than to
stay in synch with the song.

Blop. Blop. Blop. When I examined the rushes, I could just
see her mouth doing a fish-like blop, and a look of increasing
hopelessness creeping across her face. She resembled a giant
carp in a sushi bar, just selected for the table.

Then, a few weeks later, came the Velvet Underground
documentary for the *South Bank Show*. Nico had remembered
why she left modelling, why she was an unsuccessful film
actress . . . she hated the camera. Idiots pointing lenses into her,
poking away for some corny truism. Nico had a poetic sensibility, the fantastic she could happily bear, Fellini's wit and
charm, her association with Philippe Garrel, an independent
French filmmaker, both had allowed her to just get on with it,
just be herself. But having to remember lines, even her own . . .
she was just too stoned, too far out.

Nothing came out the same way twice when she was really

performing. Now that the music had begun to sound like something, she responded more to it. She actually began to *listen* occasionally to the people on stage with her. Sometimes she'd get more into listening than singing, and forget her cues. And so we started to make the songs as abstracted and free as possible, so that, at times, anyone could do anything within a certain number of bars. It made her happier and more confident on stage. But those cameras . . . When Demetrius told Nico they'd be filming her section of the documentary at the Fridge, she fell into a deep gloom.

''Ave some of the brown stuff, then top it up with a China White chaser,' suggested Echo. 'It'll just give yer that extra bit of push.'

'This isn't really Melvyn's kind of things,' said the directrice, very keen, very WASP. We'd plugged into her for a session fee so that Nico could pick up some of the white stuff, and typed out a phony bill for instrument hire.

Cale was also in town, and had been bugging everyone for 'a bit of what I like'. We'd just made an album together, a pitiful offering called *Artificial Intelligence*. The drugs, the booze, the key-jangling manager had all been present to push him to greater heights, but he just sank into a confused stupor for much of the time.

'Jim says your album's no good,' Nico told him, after which Cale had asked me to leave the studio. I was grateful to be out of it. A tired, flatulent mess of sub-Dylan lyrics written by a drinking chum, and half-assed tunes co-written by me and Dave Young. I didn't get credited properly for the songs which, retrospectively, was a blessing; and I didn't get paid properly, which was unsurprising.

Here she comes. You'd better watch your step. Nico copped her stuff and did a quick rendition of 'Femme Fatale'. The Art junkies were satisfied.

Demetrius had pressed the directrice into interviewing me as someone who could perhaps give a brief perspective on Nico's music now. I prepared a couple of things to say but, instead, they asked what influence the Velvet Underground had been on my own musical make-up. As I was only fourteen during the Summer of Love, which didn't really shine on Oldham – let alone *The Exploding Plastic Inevitable*, and all the other daffy psychedelic happenings – I couldn't give them much of an answer.

Nico reprimanded me afterwards. 'You should always have something to say.'

'I did . . . I told them I liked the clothes.'

'But didn't you say anything about the music?'

'No . . . just the clothes.'

'Don't you like the music?'

'I prefer the clothes.'

Sometimes you have to state your preferences. The brown stuff or the white.

October–November '85:

A FRIEND IN THE FOG

A new record to promote gave Nico an ostensible purpose to tour. Demetrius interpreted it to me as an obligation. Having been featured heavily on the record I was now morally obliged to support Nico and promote her career. What, I asked him, was Nico's obligation towards me? He searched for an answer. For once, Dr Demetrius was out of words. I helped him: 'Money.'

I wanted to be paid properly, as did everyone else that played with her. I'd been getting, at best, £30 a night. 'A night' means: pick up the instruments, load them, lug them; pick up the personnel; travel in discomfort, perhaps London to Glasgow; set up instruments (pianos are heavy); soundcheck (sitting around in a cold hall waiting for Nico to get herself fixed, listening to drummers 'get their sound balanced'); find hotel; gig; pack up instruments and reload them; search for all-night gas station to buy Nico's cigarettes. Sixteen hours for thirty quid.

Not enough.

Demetrius was adamant. I went to Nico – she wasn't interested, as long as she got her fifty per cent of the gig fee. Since she was already getting the publishing royalties from the album – the shows being supposedly a showcase to encourage album sales – I felt she ought to split the gig money equally between everyone.

Demetrius would say, 'But you're not famous – try doing it without her.' I'd labour the point that she was getting all the record royalties and the fan mail, which was fine. I just wanted paying.

When Demetrius fixed up an enormous tour that would include the Iron Curtain countries (except the U.S.S.R.), Northern Europe, Spain and then, possibly, Australia and Japan, I dragged my feet.

'Get another piano player to learn all the parts.'

When Nico realised that this would entail having to rehearse, work with and remunerate a total stranger, she relaxed her grip on the swag a little. We got upped to £50 per show. Big time.

Demetrius reckoned this would be the first time a non-mainstream rock act had been to the Iron Curtain. Nico was worried that she wouldn't be able to score. She knew there was some stuff around but connecting could be a problem. I reassured her that anyone who had it would come and seek her out, top junkie, Queen of the Road.

About this time I'd become involved with a Norwegian girl called Eva. It was one of those long-distance impossibilities, doomed to extinction from the start. She worked in a strip show in Stockholm, as well as turning the occasional trick if times were hard. She'd been writing and illustrating her exploits since the age of sixteen when she ran away from home in Oslo after being raped by her grandfather, a Mauthausen survivor, and had gone to live in a sex commune in Austria. My English suburban sensibility felt a bit out of step with a history like that.

The phone at Effra Road had been disconnected; Demetrius had ordered a new one under the name of Dr J. Mengele, but it hadn't been installed yet, so I was obliged to call Eva from a street payphone. I was trying to reach numbers in Stockholm and Oslo from a callbox on Brixton High Street, whamming in 50ps every ten seconds, hippies pestering me for change. Hopeless. It would be a relief to get on that tour bus.

Now that we'd become less squeamish about the Great Unmentionable (money), Demetrius gave me a rough breakdown of the tour. As the musicians' fees had been increased, economies would therefore have to be made elsewhere. One of the chief bugbears was transport hire. That could amount to around £500 a week. One ruse Demetrius had employed in the past had been to hire a bus on the understanding that it would be just for U.K. travel only . . . we'd therefore be in illegal possession of a vehicle and without the appropriate insurance. This was felt to be particularly unwise for Eastern Europe. I suggested he *buy* a bus. Vehicle hire for an eight-week tour would add up to about £4,000. He could buy a decent Talbot tourer for around £5,000. He slapped £500 down on one and off we went.

Eric Random

> Da-Ga-Di-Di   Da-Ga-Dum
> Da-Ga-Di-Di   Da-Ga-Dum
> Do Da De Ge
> Do Da De Ge

RIPPPP!

Demetrius flung the cassette to the back of the bus.

'That stuff's *dangerous!*'

We had a new recruit, a tabla player from Manchester, called Eric Random. Eric had been part of the early eighties Manchester Scene. First hanging out with Pete Shelley of the Buzzcocks, who wrote a song about him called 'What do I Get?'; then as one of Shelley's Tiller Boys; and latterly forming his own punkadelic group, Eric Random and the Bedlamites.

Eric had swung this way and that. Shelley had tried to grab his pendulum, but the little fella was hard to catch. Slippery as a tube of KY, petite, with shiny black hair and a bone structure that Vogue models would kill for, Eric would provide an essential element missing since Echo's departure – Cool. He didn't actually 'play' those tablas, nothing so crude, he seduced them as they sat coyly on a riser above the stage. First he'd remove the heavy black silk drape that protected them, then he'd shower their skins with baby talc. He'd sit cross-legged, in his own spotlight, Tantric medallion gleaming on his neck. An instant harem of adoring females would gather around his corner of the stage.

Random had spent some time in the Himalayas, smoking bongs, climbing personal mountains. He'd put himself in touch with some of the higher experiences but now he was ready to come down and get shagged.

Though Random had been talent-spotted by Demetrius, the Doctor's new protégé drove him crazy with the Indian music. He genuinely found it psychologically distressing – too linear, abstract, he liked words that you could sing along to, stuff rooted in the common clay. Great clouds of marijuana smoke would come wafting from the back of the bus as Random puffed massive lungfuls from a chillum improvised out of a Coke tin. He'd drink the Coke (breakfast), then immediately get to work bending and shaping the tin into a pipe, scraping away the paint and piercing little holes in the aluminium to accommodate the hash. One day archaeologists will be digging up Random's tins and reinterpreting them as unique counter-cultural artefacts.

Nico thought he was cute.

'Oh, Eric,' she'd say, in a singsong voice, 'have you got a little bit of haash?'

He'd give her a piece to roll one of her individual-size joints.

'You see,' she'd pointedly tell Demetrius, 'Eric knows what I need to be happy.'

We decided to decorate the new bus in a manner suited to kings of the road. We bought some stick-on girlie pinups from a French gas station, a dangling Saint Christopher and a luminous madonna, and a great Fire Eagle to stick on the bonnet. We got to the van next morning – Nico had been so incensed that for the first time in years she'd got up early and taken them all down, except for the Eagle, which couldn't be removed. Within twenty-four hours, though, she made her own contribution to the bus decor by setting her ashtray alight and burning the upholstery.

Demetrius the commander, Raincoat the driver, plus passengers Nico, me, Toby, Random and a sound engineer from Ashton-under-Lyne called Wadada. Wadada had spent a lot of time mushroom-picking up on the Saddleworth Moors. He believed that all phenomena could be divided into two categories of good and evil: 'Devil' and 'Righteous'. Meat was 'devil-food' and Nico's act was 'devil-music'. Demetrius had also taken him on as a reserve driver, but he was too short-sighted to see the road clearly. Wadada had recently been in Kingston, Jamaica, producing the great Prince Far-I, but had to return to Babylon after Prince Far-I was murdered.

En route to Yugoslavia we did a couple of warm-ups, spaced out just far enough to pay the gas, hotels and smack. The gigs were nothing special, but:

Paris

Demetrius had gone off to buy some cakes. He hated this kind of thing. Nico pressed the buzzer. The lobby door opened. Nico, Random and I entered the handsome marble foyer of an apartment block in one of the more fashionable *arrondissements*. There was a bowl of glacé mints on a smoked-glass table. Nico stubbed out her cigarette.

Mirrored lift. Bach Double Violin Concerto serenading us to the top floor.

We stood in the hallway. The fish-eye spyglass darkened for a second. Then the unlocking began. First the mortice, the bolt, then the door creaked open a couple of inches on a chain. Nico peeked her nose into the crack.

'It's me, Nico.'

The door opened on to a scene of pure devastation. What had once been a chic *pied-à-terre* for the discreet lunchtime affairs of the Parisian *haute bourgeoisie* had been reduced to a microcosm of Beirut. The walls were smoke-blackened. The curtains eaten by fire. The sofa and chairs charred and dis-embowelled. The kitchen was piled high with the solidified remains of a hundred spaghetti dinners. The sweet, pungent reek of lactic acid and stale parmesan vomit cut through the all-pervading smell of burning.

In the far corner, crouched by the gutted TV, was a woman of about twenty-five pushing forty-five. A curtain of henna'd hair half covered her face, the other half was a mass of scabs and running sores. Her arms were bare and crisscrossed with needle scars. Her legs likewise.

'Monica?' said Nico.

The girl made an effort to look up in our direction. Just then a male voice from behind us said in English, 'If you come for ze stuff zere's nossing. Ze bitch 'as 'ad it.'

A small guy in a leather blouson, with greying hair, stepped from behind the door. He strode across the room and dragged the girl to her feet by her hair. '*Salope!*' He smacked her across the face. She didn't flinch.

'Excuse me . . .' I said.

'You shoot your mouse.'

Random and I made a move towards him. He reached into his jacket and pulled out a gun, just to show us he was carrying a bit of weight, then replaced it.

'Listen,' said Random, 'we've just popped in on the off-chance, like, of a bit o' business.'

'You can shoot your fucking mouse too, ass'ole.'

'But,' Nico pleaded, 'I need to get straight . . . Monica and I will get some stuff and we'll bring some back for you too, I promise . . . just don't do that to her, pl*eease.* '

The guy still had the girl by the hair. He was thinking.

'Yes,' I said, 'that sounds like the best plan . . .'

'I sought I tell you to shoot it,' the guy snarled at me.

We all stood in silence, except the girl, who was still kneeling, still held up by her hair.

'OK' he said, 'ze chicks can go for ze stuff. You two wet 'ere.' He shoved Monica's head into his crotch. 'Don't come back empty-'anded, or shiz back on ze strit' – and threw her away from him.

Nico helped the girl to the door. As soon as they opened it, a well-groomed man in a camel coat burst in, looking around in horror. 'My God! My apartment! What have you bastards done?' (He was the landlord and had been hovering around, waiting for someone to open the door.) He ran straight over to the guy and landed him one right in the mouth. We exited with the girl.

The bus was parked on the corner across the street. 'Go!'
shouted Nico, once we were inside, 'Just go!'

Raincoat slammed his foot down and we careered off down
the blind alleys of backstreet Paris.

Nico and Monica scored off the street and had it cooked
and loaded in a jiffy. They were true professionals.

'Where's Demetrius?' I asked.

'He's still in the cakeshop,' said Toby.

We turned back to pick him up. There he was, standing
where the bus had been, looking a little lost, holding a prettily
wrapped box of cream cakes.

He jumped into the front seat, unaware of all the drama,
and opened the cakes.

'We have a guest,' I said.

Demetrius turned round, saw the girl, nodding out on
Nico's shoulder.

'Care for a chocolate éclair?' he said, offering the open box
to her. The girl lifted her head slightly, her eyes rolled up, and a
small blob of vomit, like baby puke, flopped out of her mouth.

Turned out the girl was the daughter of a South American
movie star. Like Nico, she'd been taken up by Fellini, appearing
in *Casanova*, and like Nico, she'd been dropped. Under the scabs
and scars and the sweat-matted hair were the remnants of a real
beauty. Demetrius wanted to save her. 'Let me take you away
from all this.' But to what? To a corner cupboard in Brixton with
Nico, Clarke and Echo? To a death worse than fate?

The next show was in the gingerbread town of Nuremberg in
southern Germany. Needless to say we had to go and see the
Zeppelinwiese Stadium, Hitler's biggest gig. It was a huge
amphitheatre, once a Zeppelin landing field, redesigned by Albert
Speer, that in 1938 could hold a quarter of a million men and
seventy thousand spectators. Indeed, the whole town had been
one big rallying point, with one and a half million visitors for the
Greatest Show on Earth. Hitler would deliver apoplectic rants
from the podium (still there) that overlooked the parade ground.

The Nazi insignia have all been torn down, of course,
although the impress of huge imperial eagles can still be

detected in the pseudo-classicism of the arena, and the great bronze doors out of which the Führer would step to greet the massed multitudes still remain, scratched with graffiti, crude swastikas, 'Walthamstow Boot Boys', 'Adolf loves Eva '39', that kind of thing.

Needless to say everyone had their snapshot taken on Hitler's podium, except for Demetrius who, unable to leave the protective shadow of the bus, stood by the driver's door in case a sudden Nazi renaissance required a quick Diaspora. Nico just stayed in her seat and whacked up a big one.

That night as we slept on crisp cotton sheets, white as a starched dirndl, Demetrius had the first of a number of fits that were to plague him throughout the tour. He said he could only think of Julius Streicher, Hitler's Whipmaster General, stalking the town with his bullwhip, clearing it of Jews, like the medieval falconers who prepared the Emperor's progress, flushing out the rats from his path.

Nico was as sympathetic as ever: 'Why don't you just go home?'

'And rid the sacred German soil of the Eternal Jew?'

Nico shook her head. He always had to drag it down to the grudge level of national stereotypes.

'Give me a child till the age of seven – I quote Ignatius Loyola – and he is mine for life,' said Demetrius. 'Hitler also employed that motto, Nico . . . when were you born? 1938? Let me see . . . forty-five minus thirty-eight why, that makes seven. Interesting.'

Demetrius decided he could do without Nico for a day and hired a Merc. Toby and I joined him. We fancied following him on his private tour of provincial cakeshops. Within ten minutes he'd damaged the car, his nerves were so bad. The bonnet wouldn't close. We chugged off at the nearest Ausfahrt and found a cakeshop. For half an hour we sat there cakeless while the Goyim stared us out.

Back at the car rental Toby and I sat on the bonnet while Demetrius went to the office to hand them the keys. As soon as he came out we all ran for it, the bonnet yawning wide open: *Deutschland Erwache!*

'Tabla player?' said Raincoat. 'Table tapper, more like . . . is there anybody there? I can't fookin' 'ear 'im.'

Pit-a-pat-pat and Toby's Big Bang.

'Why can't we have a bass player?' I asked Demetrius.

'Nico likes him . . . he looks good.'

Immediately we got into Yugoslavia, Nico and Random started fretting about the drugs.

'Not my problem,' said Demetrius. 'Adventure ahead . . . Conquistadors of the open road!'

'We come in search of cakes,' said Raincoat.

We pulled up for fuel. The bus took diesel. Demetrius jumped out and shoved the nozzle into the tank and left it to feed from the bottle while he walked off . . . to find some cakes. Raincoat opened the sliding door, shouted to Demetrius to come and keep hold of it. Demetrius immediately self-inflated to bursting point. Raincoat was a mere minion.

'Don't talk to me about filling up, I know all about filling up, when you've been on the road as long as I have then. . .'

The nozzle sprang out of the tank, a writhing spitting snake of diesel. Demetrius tried to catch it but the thing was alive and wriggling furiously out of his reach. He grabbed it but stumbled, the head flipped round in his hands, and so it was that Dr Demetrius went down on the diesel. The spouting beast pumped into his mouth. Demetrius gagged and pulled away, throwing the engorged head blindly across the forecourt and into the open bus, soaking Wadada. Motorists ran for cover, grabbing their children. People were screaming. All except Nico, who just sat there staring fixedly at the empty road ahead and lit up another Marlboro.

The Yugoslavian gigs invited the truly exotic. For instance, a girl came to the Zagreb concert who'd been kicked out of her village for being a witch. Her best friend had committed suicide and they'd blamed it on her. She had the looks of a heartbreaker. Demetrius and Wadada immediately started fighting over her. Her complete indifference to them sent them into frenzies of credit-card lust.

At dinner Demetrius tried to impress Esmeralda with his knowledge of fine wines. His fingers ran up and down the list until he spotted a word he recognised. 'I think we'll have the Riesling.' The girl threw a black glance at him with her dark eyes as he was about to taste it. He coughed, choked and spat it out.

''E prefers diesel,' said Raincoat to the waiter. 'Yer wouldn't 'ave any Château Esso, by any chance?'

The little witch wanted to return with us to the West, but we were going east, to Belgrade and then up into Hungary. She'd have to hitch a ride on another broomstick.

To rid the bus of the smell of diesel we drove with the sliding door open. This irritated Nico as she couldn't relight her dimps properly. The temperature was in the 80s as we drove to Belgrade. Demetrius was sweating it out in the thermal underwear his mother had given him and which out of duty he had to wear under his worsted three-piece and trilby. It was harvest time and the corn was being hung up to dry. The main roads were empty, but we'd still get stuck behind corn-carrying tractors. I suggested we take a side road as nothing could be as slow as these tractors – until we got stuck behind a corn-carrying horse and cart.

We drove along dirt roads, through villages with small squat houses, wooden roofs and white plaster walls with corn hanging up to dry. Oxen would stray into our path. Our progress was so slow that people started coming out of their houses to greet us. Women in headscarves, little boys in short trousers and girls in white communion dresses. They'd rush up to give us sweetmeats, candied fruit, sugared pieces of orange and plums. I didn't know if they thought we were something special or whether they were just kinder than we were.

I wanted to get away from the bus for a few minutes, just to touch another reality for a moment. At the next gas station I legged it across the road to a wayside cafe. I ordered a beer and a slivovitz. There was only one other guy at the bar. His Lada was parked alongside the window in full view. There was a coffin in the back. I asked him who it was. He couldn't speak English so I pointed. 'Mama,' he said.

Away from the hermetically sealed, artificial climate of the tour bus, life (and death) gently slapped you in the face to remind you of their omnipresence.

In Ljubljana we picked up a gypsy. At least she said she was a gypsy, and that was good enough for Toby. He had it all mapped out: the caravan, the fortune-telling booth. All she wanted was a ride to Austria. We'd already tried to cross into Hungary from Yugoslavia but they'd turned us back. (We only had holiday visas . . . so why, then, did we have a drum kit in the back?)

'She's sitting in my seat,' said Nico, offended by the gypsy's free and easy air. Nico wouldn't actually address the girl directly but complained instead to Toby. 'Come on – get her out!' (Nico's Central European peasant blood made her afraid of gypsies; plus, of course, there were the health warnings from Dr Goebbels.)

The gypsy had never heard of Nico, she'd just come along to the club to see a Western act play, tag along, and fuck her way west. Have cunt will travel.

Toby pulled her into the back seat with him, but she couldn't keep still and started wandering up and down the bus.

'Tell her to fucking sit down, or I'll kill her,' shouted Nico. The girl couldn't hear Nico as she was listening to Wadada's Prince Far-I tape on a Walkman and chewing gum.

'Fer a pair of nylons she'll suck yer dick all the way back ter Wythenshawe,' said Raincoat.

We tried the cheap places in Vienna, but Demetrius scorned them. Nico didn't give a shit, she just wanted somewhere warm with a bed, now that the nights were getting cold and the dealers hiding in their nests. Demetrius booked us into the Regina on his American Express card. The gypsy danced with joy. What the fuck was *this*? A little piece of heaven on the ground. She wanted to try everything. As soon as she got into Toby's room she called room service. Toby just waved the flunkeys in, champagne buckets, plates of smoked salmon, *petits fours* on silver platters. A couple of hours later there was a frenzied knocking at my door. I was taking a shower, dripping in my towel when I answered. It was the gypsy. She waltzed in, wearing a Nico T-shirt and nothing else.

'I can do deep throat,' she said, and whisked away the

towel. Within seconds she was into her party piece. 'This isn't such a good idea.' She couldn't answer. I suggested she should go back to Toby's room.

'Should I get another girl?' she asked. 'I can do that . . . I can make girls do anything I want.'

Next day as she waved goodbye to us on the hotel steps, Nico asked Toby, 'Did you make her cry? You should make *all* the girls cry.'

'Did you make her cry?' became a running epigraph to such brief liaisons. 'If Nico had been a male she'd have made the girls cry,' pontificated Demetrius. She loved the idea of the punishment fuck. The warm, hugging stuff wasn't really to her taste. It was all a memory now anyway.

'Of course it's her own sexuality she's denying,' he continued. Did I know that she'd been raped as a teenager in Berlin?

I didn't.

Nico was working as a temp for the U.S. Air Force. A black American sergeant had raped not only her but other girls under his employ. She'd kept quiet about it, but he was found out and court-martialled. She had to testify for the prosecution at his trial. He was sentenced to death and shot. Nico was fifteen.

'Not only does she have to carry the horror of the rape but the secret guilt of somehow being complicit, by her testimony, in his execution. Sex, for Nico,' said Demetrius as we left Bergasse Strasse, 'is irrevocably associated with punishment.'

Pecs, Hungary

Nico and Random were whingeing and wheedling, winding down the spiral staircase into pre-withdrawal panic tantrums. They weren't actually out of dope, but they only had crumbs left and they were a thousand miles from home.

People say you can't become addicted to marijuana. Random proved himself to be an exception to this rule. He'd smoked it every day for the past ten years, since he was fourteen. He'd never been so far away from a source.

Nico was threatening to call off the tour if she didn't get more stuff soon.

I was consulting with Demetrius in his room about the best course of action. The phone would ring – alternately Nico and Random, each with a new and even more valid reason for not going on. With Nico it always came down to the smack, we knew it, she knew it, and she was utterly straight about it. Gear = go. With pot-heads, though, I've found they always try to think up some other justification outside themselves for doing nothing. (Coke-users, on the other hand, are game for anything – they just have to go to the toilet first.) There's a self-fulfilling honesty, though, about heroin-users. They can't pretend so easily as their habit is so obvious. The junkie's dishonesty comes in always trying to find someone else to blame for their habit.

Demetrius and I wanted to continue the tour. So did Raincoat and Toby and Wadada. The shows had been interesting, audiences were curious. At first they weren't so sure about what was going on. As ever they expected the living ghosts of the Velvet Underground. Piano, drums and tabla were an unusual combination of instruments for them, as well as for me. But perhaps Nico's harmonium-centred wailing struck deeper ancestral chords and by the end of the performances they'd warmed up a bit. (If anyone can actually warm to a Nico song.)

Demetrius and I formed a delegation to Nico's room. Raincoat was reluctant to join us. Although he wanted to stay on the tour, he'd also been 'knockin' on Nico's door' and had thus partially contributed to her depleted circumstances. He did, however, assure us that he'd do his utmost to sniff something out as soon as we got to Budapest.

Demetrius told Nico she had to continue. He made all sorts of thinly veiled threats concerning broken contracts. The more he threatened the more stubborn she became. When the legal stuff failed, he tried to get her to reconsider on moral and professional grounds. The only way to her, though, was to worm in with some sort of flattery, build her up, make her feel the fans' disappointment. She agreed to stick it out a bit longer. She had three or four shots left, which she could eke out further with some of Demetrius's valium, and then there were her cottons. Random's calls for mutiny went silent when he heard that the Good Ship Nico would steam on.

As soon as we got to Budapest the poor promoter was hammered into a corner by Nico and Random. Could he get this, could he get that? He was only a young operator, called Chabbi, still a student, he thought it was a BYO party, he hadn't realised he had to supply the refreshments as well. He came back with a few tabs of codeine and some pal's straggly dope plant, still in its pot. Nico necked the pills, Random grabbed the plant, stripped it down to its sad little stalks, and within seconds he was puffing away on his coke-tin, trying to get high on slow-burning nothing.

Chabbi had booked us into the local hostel, the Citadel, a converted hilltop fortress overlooking the city. The place had a splendid view of the city, but 'not a fit spot ter feather down,' said Toby. We stayed one night, during which Demetrius went to a private sex show with Chabbi, had another fit, and awoke covered in blood. We never saw Chabbi again.

In the distance Demetrius and I could see the glass-domed roof of the Hotel Gellert. We booked ourselves in. The glass dome opens so that the sun's rays can shine down on an ornate swimming-pool with marble lions spouting water. There were plunges, Turkish baths, massage. For a grooming fetishist, a paradise. Of no interest whatsoever to Nico, for whom it would have been a torture chamber.

I decided Demetrius was my ally for this tour. Our addiction was to adventure and Nico could work it out for herself.

The Road to Romance

We got into Czechoslovakia by the skin of our teeth. The border control saw the instruments and Demetrius nearly blew it for us by saying we were jazz musicians, in the hope that we'd sound more innocent. But the Czech régime didn't dig Miles. It had become their recent policy to ban jazz and imprison its practitioners.

Brno (where they manufactured the Bren gun) conformed much more to preconceived notions of life in the Eastern bloc – a sulphurous yellow light, barely illuminating empty and dusty streets. Fear. Everyone in uniform. Our conspicuousness increased our latent paranoia.

It felt good, though. It might seem a gratuitous reflection on other people's suffering, but there *was* a tension here that was missing in the West. For a start, the people had strong faces, they looked like individuals, which is another thing we don't see much of in the West. Telly and Pop sugar us up so much we still look like babies.

It was a pleasure to find my hotel room rather amateurishly bugged. And the patched sheets, cold radiators and smell of cheap disinfectant gave it that authentic penitential feel, not unlike, I imagine, an English public school.

Demetrius tried to contact our promoter in Prague, Miloscz, who every day had a different office number. 'Nico needs something, or we can't do the tour.'

'What does she need?' Miloscz didn't know.

'Fuel. Nico needs *special fuel* to keep her wheels rolling.'

Miloscz understood. We had to meet him third traffic-light after the interchange coming into Prague from the Brno road.

True to his promise, Miloscz was waiting at the appointed spot. We pulled into the hard shoulder. He beckoned a couple of us to get out. Behind a hedge he'd hidden a cache of petrol cans. Nico's 'fuel'. He'd interpreted Demetrius's coded message literally and assumed Nico wanted paying in petrol.

What she needed was heroin, Demetrius explained.

'Heroin?? My God!' Miloscz didn't know what to say. Why had we asked for fuel? Heroin? He didn't want to, couldn't possibly, have anything to do with heroin.

We took the petrol anyway, as Miloscz said we could exchange it later for diesel.

Demetrius asked which hotel we were booked in.

Hotel? Miloscz could help us find one, maybe, but hadn't Nico's agency already fixed that?

We followed his car into the centre of Prague while Demetrius explained the situation to Nico. My heart went out to him as he told her that the petrol cans sloshing around her feet represented her performance fee and that the heroin would not be forthcoming. As the bus rolled into Wenceslas Square Nico was at her wits' end. She had nothing left and no one cared.

We parked up outside the elegant Hotel Europa and watched the Russian soldiers' dismal foot patrol, followed by the occasional rusty armoured car. They were square-bashing the Czechs into submission. The oppression wasn't so much hostile as omnivorously boring. The spotty toy soldiers didn't want to be there, and the people didn't want them there. For the heart of a city it sure was quiet. There were a couple of stalls selling pickled slices of some indeterminate grey fish. Apart from occasional pairs of old ladies with empty shopping bags, everyone seemed to be somehow alone. I realised when we'd all climbed out of the van that we were, in the eyes of a totalitarian régime, what constituted a crowd.

As we were directly in front of the Europa, Nico assumed it must be our hotel, and began lugging her bag towards the entrance. When Demetrius pointed out that we weren't actually staying there, that we didn't, in fact, have any place to stay, she gave him a mighty kick in the balls, a steel-capped castrating avenger. When the heroin was out, Nico always seemed to get sudden bursts of energy.

Demetrius doubled up, gasping for breath, his hands cupping what was left of his retracted testicles. Miloscz immediately disappeared. Passers-by smirked, but didn't stop. The soldiers expressed a slight consternation as they goosestepped past, but they didn't stop either. Nothing could alter the mechanical rhythm of the city's artificial heart.

'This is *my* tour,' screamed Demetrius, emptying a bottle of valium into his hand. '. . . *Mine*. She can go!'

What Nico had done, in her tantrum of self-absorption, was to inject a small shot of human emotion into the bloodstream of that tragic paralysed city.

*

Miloscz was a bag of nerves. A Czech version of Paolo Bendini. Same lack of a haircut, same TopoGigio mouse expression. A fan, with no previous experience of the wrong end of Nico's boot, he helped us to find a couple of hotels. The East Germans were having a public holiday and they'd all flooded into Prague; most places were full, so we'd have to split up. Nico on her own – quarantined and caged; the rest of us divided around the square.

Demetrius asked Miloscz where the venue was.

Venue? Maybe it was at a colliery about twenty kilometres east of the city . . . he'd have to check.

Now his myriad phone numbers and addresses began to divulge their secret meaning. Miloscz was a man on the move, one step ahead of the secret police. The police were secret, so everything else in Czech life had to be. The venue was a closely guarded secret that even Miloscz would only know at the last minute.

We drove out to the colliery, down mud tracks, past smoking slagheaps. Miloscz was waiting outside, waving at us to stop. The gig had been relocated to the university, but he had some more diesel for us if we wanted to swap the petrol.

Nico was groaning and sweating, spitting a constant bile of hate, mostly in Demetrius's direction. He accused her of Jew-baiting.

'I am not your whipping-boy,' he kept repeating.

We drove up to the campus. Miloscz stopped us by a wall. He urged us to be quick. We had to haul our instruments over the wall and into the nearest lecture theatre.

The place was full to bursting, the audience banked up vertically on desks so that we were nose to nose. We had to set up in front of them. There was no stage, no P.A. system, no lights other than the overhead striplighting, and no time to indulge ourselves in a soundcheck. We just plugged in and began.

The audience seemed to plug in immediately as well. They didn't need warming up, they weren't going to be coy with us. Nico let fly with pure screams, shredding her lyrics to pieces. We'd played for maybe twenty-five minutes when Miloscz gave us the sign to quit. The audience stamped their feet, yelled and applauded, thanked us, shaking our hands as they left. I think in that twenty-five minutes we'd all probably concentrated the best we had in us.

We hurriedly packed our instruments. The students kindly carried them down the corridor to the waiting bus for us. I got delayed talking to someone, hungry to pick my brains on some musical point or other. I'd never experienced, before or since, such interest and enthusiasm, such belief in the redemptive power of music.

As I was catching up with the rest, I cast a glance into one of the classrooms. A guy in a shiny grey suit had a hold of Miloscz by the hair and was banging his head against the blackboard. I stopped in my tracks. The door slammed shut in my face. Someone grabbed my arm – it was the student I'd just been talking to. He bundled me off to the safety of the bus.

We debated what to do – stay or go? Raincoat and Nico would remain in the bus while the rest of us went back to see what, if anything, we could do. A large crowd had gathered in the foyer, buzzing about the gig. We pushed abruptly past them to try and find Miloscz, but he was gone.

Next day, as we were drinking tea and eating ersatz cream cakes in the Europa's café, Miloscz walked in with two cans of diesel. His face was half hanging off. One of his eyes completely closed, the other cut and blackened.

He explained that the concert had been illegal from the start. The police had been following him continuously for days – the coalmine had been a detour to try and throw them off. He was sorry for the deception, but he hadn't wanted to alarm us or discourage us from playing. He was sorry too that Nico was unwell, but he didn't know anything about heroin or where to get it. He hoped she/all of us would accept his apologies for the apparent disorganisation. If he'd booked hotels in advance for us that would have alerted the police sooner and we wouldn't have even got into the country.

'This music – dark music – is not popular with Authorities.'

We stuffed him full of tea and cakes and asked him if he wanted to come with us for a drive (we were getting insecure away from the bus). Nico was staying in her hotel, she was too sick.

'Fuck her,' said Demetrius. Miloscz looked surprised.

'Nico is difficult artist to work with?' he asked.

'First of all, let's get our lexical definitions straight, Miloscz,' said Demetrius, still wounded by Nico's castration attempt. 'I think we can safely subtract the noun "artist" and the verb "work" from that sentence. Nico is an ar-sehole rather than an ar-tist, and she's never done an honest day's work in her life.'

'Yeh, but,' Raincoat intervened on behalf of his patroness, 'she's never pulled a gig yet.'

True, true, everyone nodded.

'OK, then,' said Demetrius to Miloscz, 'let's just say . . . Nico is a difficult arsehole to work with, and leave it at that.'

As we set off with Miloscz in the bus, we noticed a rather grand fifties black saloon quite blatantly pull out behind us. Miloscz informed us that it was the cops in the shiny suits who'd 'interviewed' him the previous evening.

As we pottered about the countryside north of Prague (the black saloon sulking close behind) we couldn't figure out why there were fields of vegetables yet none in the restaurants and shops. (Nico's vegetarianism meant she'd been subsisting on a wartime ration of carob chocolate and Europa cakes.)

'All exported to Germany and Nederlands,' said Miloscz.

'Doesn't seem right, some'ow,' said Toby.

'Perhaps is for the best,' said Miloscz. 'All vegetables contain double permitted levels of cadmium, lead and mercury. It's better you eat only cakes.' He chuckled, wincing with the pain in his jaw.

In the evening we went to a hotel disco – the shiny suits followed us. It was the kind of place where you get fat sausage-eating German tourists and hookers with Kathy Kirby makeup, as well as the straightforward package tourists. Demetrius perked up.

'Have you noticed how much happier we all are when Nico isn't around?' he asked. We half-heartedly agreed, but the truth was we all loved to watch the fights. They were like a bad marriage – compellingly awful.

Demetrius and Raincoat fancied a spin on the dance-floor with the 'ladies'. Raincoat sidled up to one. He pointed at her.

'Are you . . .' then he pointed to himself '. . . fer me?'

The girl smiled sweetly. Raincoat shouted over the music. 'Right then . . . 'ow much?' He wanted to get down to business quickly. The girl didn't quite understand. He pointed at her again. 'For *you* . . . 'ow much? . . . dollaris? . . . monneta?' Deeply offended and hurt, she gave Raincoat a slap across the face. She was just an East German student on a cultural trip to Prague, definitely not on the game. Her parents came up looking worried, the shiny suits were agitatedly conferring amongst themselves. Miloscz slipped out. Without Nico's sweetly civilising influence we were just English yobs abroad.

On our last morning in Prague we had nothing to spend our Czech koruna on, so we bought up lots of 'authentic Bohemian black glass' jewellery made from King Wenceslas's glass eye.

Miloscz turned up with goodbye gifts of diesel for us. Hugs and kisses and useless addresses. The shiny suits looked on as we packed the van with yet more cans of fuel. There was nowhere to put our feet, so our knees were up near our chins. Nico was deeply miserable. She'd developed a suppurating abscess on her leg and spent most of her time swabbing and dressing it.

We rolled off slowly down the square, the diesel glugging ominously with every bump and lurch along the unsurfaced road. A bomb on wheels.

The black saloon followed us dutifully a few paces behind. Raincoat clocked them in the mirror.

''Ave they got nothin' better ter do?' He scrambled around in the glove compartment for a cassette, whipping through the selections, and finally settling on one. Then, joining up with the slow patrol of military, secret police and German tourist coaches, he took us on a final circuit of Wenceslas Square. The windows down, he turned Ol' Blue Eyes up full. Russian would be a crime – 'cos Nice 'n' Easy did it every time.

*

We briefly interrupted the Eastern Bloc tour to play a few dates in Scandinavia. The gigs were a dispiriting flop, after the enthusiasm we'd encountered in the East. Nico had hit them the year before – once was enough.

While we were in Oslo I looked up my own Nordic goddess, Eva. I had a lot of hopes pinned on the meeting, despite the 'Dear Bjorn' letter I'd received a couple of months back. She didn't show up at the gig, as it hadn't been advertised, so the next day I stayed behind with Demetrius and Nico (who was sick). I went to Eva's apartment block (where Edvard Munch once had a small studio – it had retained that tortured vibe) in the old Christiania part of Oslo. The place was being rebuilt. I asked a guy downstairs if he knew where Eva was. He showed me to another dungeonesque wing of the old grey building. I knocked – no one there. So I left a note.

'Hello, bastard,' she said as we met outside a pink-and-white American ice-cream parlour in the Karl Johan square. We found a corner in a nearby bar. Over brandy at £10 a shot, she fixed those ice-blue eyes on me and spelt out in block capitals how, while working at the strip joint in Stockholm, she'd got close to the other girls there. *VERY CLOSE.* She thought women were better to be with, more understanding. 'Anyway. What is it you men want from us? It's just a *hole* – no?'

I tried to get a cab back to the hotel. In my idiot joy at hearing Eva's voice on the phone I'd rushed out in what I had on – a thin jacket and shirt. A great neon sign above the square flashed, as if in pride, 0°C. The Norsemen were at their revels and the taxi queue was endless. I was trembling so much from the cold and the self-pity that I just curled up on the pavement. A stranger gave me his cab and I made it back to the Hotel West, where I defrosted my misery in great pools to Demetrius. 'Who can comment accurately on these foolish, complicated things?' he said. 'But it's clear she won't have you any more – so, here, take two of these and go to bed.' He handed me his own personal bottle of valium.

Next morning, still woozy from the valium and with my broken heart tied to a ball and chain behind me, I dragged myself on to the Oslo–Stockholm train with Nico and

Demetrius. This is one of the world's great train rides, over the mountains, looking out across the fjords. The carriages are laid out like drawing-rooms with sofas and armchairs and magazines to read. 'Go away!' said Nico to a friendly steward offering her a complimentary newspaper. Then she scowled at me and turned on Demetrius. 'What's the matter with him, blubbering away like that? Pay more attention to *me*! Jesus . . . I need a *shot*!'

'You certainly do, my dear,' whispered Demetrius as the other passengers turned round, 'right between the eyes. Can't you see the boy's upset?'

'Over some silly little whore . . .'

Later, when she'd got herself straight, Nico sluiced her syringe clean, squirting a needle jet of bloody water into her mouth. 'Jim . . . why do you get so upset? You know women *are* inferior.'

We rolled off the boat into the grim and sullen port of Gdansk. As we drove to Warsaw through a unique topography of puddles, empty dirt roads, cabbage fields and extinct Nazi deathcamps, a perpetual grey fog, like battle smoke, never lifted. The war was still on in Poland.

(We'd come the hard way from Malmö, Sweden, in a decrepit tub – incredibly called the *Vulva* – stinking of shipgrease, oil and disinfectant. There was a bar on the boat, the Sky Bar, that sold only vodka and took only hard currency. It had a disco, about six foot square. Apart from the magnificent seven of us, there were just a couple of other people in the bar, both of them hookers. The moment we sat down one of them got up from her stool and started a hideous fertility dance alone in the disco spotlight. A massive, treetrunk-legged escapee from an agricultural collective, she'd clearly received her sexual education bending over in the fields, planting potatoes, boared like a sow from behind. Her cheeks were ruddy with broken veins, her mouth thin and mean like a peasant. She looked like she knew how to wring a chicken's neck. She stomped about to an Abba song while we looked on. Demetrius fancied a go, just to outrage Nico. 'It'll be like fuckin' a bucket,' said Raincoat.)

Wadada had a cassette of Fauré's *Requiem*, for which he was working out a Dub version. Demetrius was less than enraptured.

'Has somebody died?' he asked Wadada. Demetrius had a very honest and pragmatic approach to music – meaning was derived from context, everything had its place. Requiems did not belong in a Talbot tour bus. He proposed Country & Western, which was made for the road. No one wanted it. Random offered to put on a tabla exposition, recorded live in Benares. Nope. We sat in silence.

Nico was still exiled in her special seat in the bus, ashtray overflowing, wrapped up in a patchwork sheepskin jacket, silent and withdrawn. The fog rolled by. We'd wipe the condensation from the windows, but there was nothing to see and nowhere to stop and eat, just grey fading into black.

Then lights started to appear in the blackness, figures, more lights. We'd drive on. The gathering of lights increased, we could begin to distinguish people, faces illuminated by candlelight, gravestones. We reasoned, as it was November 2, that it must be All Souls' Night. In Poland, perhaps, the dead have more significance than the living. We drove on through dark and empty villages, to find, on the outskirts, the graveyards alight with humanity. It continued for a couple of hours, and even when the friends of the dead had dispersed the candles were left burning on the graves. Then it was black night again.

Suddenly Nico leapt from her seat. 'Look! It's Jim!' She peered into the rolling fog. 'I can see him. . .'

'Jim's 'ere, in the back,' said Toby. 'Aren't yer, Jim?'

I reassured Nico I was there.

'No-o-o. No-o-o . . . not *you*, Jim.' Nico continued staring into the night. 'Jim *Morrison* . . . I can see him . . . there . . . loook!' She pointed out into the empty fog.

We all strained to see.

'Where?' asked Toby.

'Can't see fook,' said Raincoat.

We carried on trying to discern the lead singer of the Doors out there in the nothingness.

''Ang on,' said Wadada, squinting through his bifocals. 'I think I might 'ave clocked a visage . . .'

Sure enough, it was the Lizard King himself, a-writhin' around in his black leathers, sucking off the mike, dancing us all into an early grave. Like him, we'd all died and been sent to Poland for our purple sins.

Joy awaited Nico in Warsaw in the form of a horse needle and a bottle of 'kompot'. Kompot, so-called because it resembles a drink made from a compote of mixed fruit, is actually a kind of opium vodka, distilled from poppy heads. Poles (check your local deli) like to eat bread with poppy seeds sprinkled on top, and poppy seed cake (a kind of marble cake with poppy seed veins). Such eating habits support a sub-economy of kompot distillers, all of whom are addicts or 'narkomanis' themselves.

'It's the best hit I've ever had,' said Nico, overjoyed to be back in a cultural milieu she recognised . . . The Living Dead.

The rest of us would have been happy with just a few of the poppy seed cakes, as we still hadn't eaten anything other than a sandwich made from kabanos sausage – 'devil food,' said Wadada.

We played the same hall they use for the international Chopin competition and I used the same piano. In fact there was a bewildering choice of four Steinway concert grands. It was an absurdly grandiose and formal setting for our small thing and our performance was consequently as reserved as the seats. The audience applauded politely and looked on, serious and subdued. I think the problem was that, for once, Nico was out-doomed. It was a relief to get back to the kompot in the dressing room, where the promoter was waiting with another kabanos sausage each for us. He was another Miloscz/Bendini type. I had them narrowed down by now. They were the brainy loners – their career opportunities would exist either in serial-killing or pop promotion.

Zbigniev, 'Ziggy', had a zit problem. Nico offered to squeeze them for him.

'Wow! My God!! To be hearink zuch think from Nico, Welvet Undergron Warhola Zuperztar.'

Ziggy paid us about ten million zlotys each and then took us to our hotel for a 'zpecial' hello/goodbye/thankyou zupper.

A crowd was gathered around the bus, and after we were jostled and thanked and shaken and pressed we realised we'd all been dipped. Just little things – Walkmans, cigarettes, Eric Random's hair-gel and eyeliner.

We followed Ziggy and his pals as they drove us through the 1950s time tunnel cold war ambience. You could almost hear the pompous synthesizer music and the brooding po-faced commentary.

Ziggy pulled up about twenty yards from the hotel. He wouldn't be coming in, he wasn't allowed . . . foreigners and nationals couldn't fraternise in the international hotels. He realised it was the first opportunity we'd had for a decent meal since Sweden, so he'd wait outside for us. We watched Ziggy and his pals hanging around outside smoking while we broke our fillings on pieces of shot from the wild pheasant.

Next morning Demetrius showed up, ashen grey. He'd been wandering the streets since dawn, where the old ghetto had been, talking with 'the ghosts of my people'.

Nico was trying to be friends again. Happy on the kompot, she'd begun to notice the existence of others and her abscess was beginning to heal. The horse needle had helped her to draw off the pus. 'Look!' she said to Demetrius, holding up the syringe for his approval, like a kid with her potty, 'two ccs!'

'My God, Nico . . . I think you must inhabit a separate reality from the rest of us.' Demetrius shoved his Vick inhaler up one nostril. 'I've just spent the morning breathing in the dust of 400,000 murdered innocents.'

She didn't understand. Her leg was getting better. The kompot was great. She'd be in good shape for Berlin . . . Ghetto?

Berlin, Latin Quarter

'All Tomorrow's Parties' — a capella.

```
. . . - / - - - - - - - - - - / - - - - - -,
- / - - - - — - - — - - - / - - - -,
- - / - - - - / and / - - - - - / - - - / - - - - - - - - . . .
- - -'- - / - - - - - - - / - - - - / - - / - - - - - - - / - - - - - -!
```
[Permission to reproduce lyrics refused]

. . . 'You're staring down my fucking throoaat!' Nico broke off mid-song to deal with a vampette who'd been locked on her every move. She had the audience totally intimidated — which is exactly what they'd paid for. (In contrast to the last time we'd played Berlin.) Again it wasn't the music, but the vibe people came to pick up on. If you were a happy, well-adjusted, straight-ahead, thinking, caring sort of person, then you'd probably be satisfied with a sermon and blessing from Sting. If you were totally fucked, you were probably at the Latin Quarter.

We had to drive from Berlin to Rotterdam in one day. As all motorists had to observe the speed limit down the corridor it would mean an eight- or ten-hour journey. We were doing OK until we hit a tailback, north of Hanover. The truckers were holding a lightning strike across northern Germany, and were blocking the autobahn lanes.

We sat, waited and debated. Random jumped out and with his pocket knife tried to stab the tyres of an articulated lorry. It was about as effective as a mosquito biting the leg of an elephant. We waited. Demetrius decided he was going to get us out of this jam and to the gig on time. 'Don't they realise we're entertainers? We can't disappoint our public, we have a duty to the audience which far exceeds our responsibility to the German economy.' He pulled us off on to the hard shoulder. The other motorists scowled at us, but before long we had a beat-up old white Audi following us full of Turkish *Gast-arbeiter*. This infuriated the truckers even more, and they blocked off the hard shoulder. A motorist got out of his VW, a slightly hippy type in a lilac duvet coat, and banged on the window. Demetrius wound it down.

'You vill stop please and svitch off your engine! Ve don't vont your pollution!'

Demetrius looked at him and slowly wound the window up in his face. 'Even the environmentalists are only obeying orders.' He revved the engine and turned off on to the grass verge. It was now dark, and I prayed Demetrius wouldn't drive us into a ditch. We lumbered on at a tilt for a few kilometres, until the next exit, where we pulled off on to a small road. It was badly lit and we had no idea where we were. We drove around, probably in circles, for about half an hour, until we came to an abrupt halt before a roadsign which read 'Bergen Belsen'. No one said anything. Demetrius just turned the bus round and we headed back to the autobahn, tucking ourselves discreetly into the mainstream of the body politic.

Amsterdam: Paradise Regained

As ever, you couldn't find anywhere to sit in the dressing-room at the Paradiso. Most of the seats were taken by girlies, queue-ing up for Eric Random's Tantric Love Juice. There was an anorexic poet called Arnaud who looked like a pierrot in a baggy white suit. He did press-ups in the middle of the floor while reciting his poems in Dutch. Nico and her group were incidental. Demetrius would let anyone he wanted in now, it was his tour. Some kind of turning-point had been reached in Eastern Europe.

'I give therefore I am,' he would say, and invite strangers to help themselves to our drinks. *His* tour, *his* party, *his* choice of companions. Nico had suddenly become extraneous, a walk-on in her own movie, carrying a hypodermic needle. The music became even more marginalised. If Nico couldn't be congenial towards her host then she could 'bug off'.

Dr Demetrius seemed to have grown taller and expanded even further in status. His tie was straight again. His hat fitted at last. His fits had abated, his debilitating agoraphobia held at bay. 'Yes, James,' he would say, 'a man needs to keep a grip on his own potential, and not become deflected from his higher purpose in life by the mean-spirited and ungenerous, such as Fraulein Christa Paffgen.'

'I like Nico,' I said, 'she's OK . . . she's funny . . .' It didn't sound like much of a defence, but then I didn't feel that Nico needed defending.

'A person only begins to become an individual when they cease to be the victim of their own temperament,' said Demetrius. 'Nico is, ultimately, despite her amusement value, a parasite.'

'In that case,' I said, 'we're all parasitising ourselves by working with her.'

'Wherefore such cynicism, James? Do I not detect in your tone the chaise-longued ennui of the Oxford common-room? You misunderstand me, I also like – love – Nico. But I know what she is.'

'What's that then? You're hip to her secrets?'

'Not especially – though occasional confidences have been placed with me, I feel that there are no great disclosures awaiting us that will suddenly reveal a deeply warm and caring human being. With Nico I feel that what you see is what you get.'

'That's OK by me,' I said. 'There's a kind of purity in her . . . in that remorseless monomania, that heroic indifference. Nico wouldn't piss on us if we were on fire, so at least we know where we stand. The problem is, you wanted her to love you, and she can't, so you're disappointed.'

'I wanted love, certainly, but I feel that Nico also needs love, despite herself. I think we all of us need to divest ourselves of who or what we think we are, to risk a certain nakedness.'

'Perhaps some people look better with their inhibitions on?' I suggested.

Demetrius shook his head. 'Why is it, James, that you favour the smart riposte at the expense of authentic feeling? Dear God! The great Zero that lies at the heart of every Englishman. It's an emptiness he tries to fill with breeding, an Oxbridge education and the cultivation of influential friends, but none of this can disguise his essential poverty in matters of the heart.'

Such were the thoughts of Dr Demetrius before Raincoat poisoned him.

We met Raincoat in one of those dope-shop/coffee-bars that stink of hippy paranoia. Demetrius stood there in his double-breasted suit and trilby – his incongruity filling the place up. He considered drug-taking a vulgar high and any form of drug dependency the sign of a weak personality. Unfortunately, though, Demetrius had not managed to curb his addiction to cakes. Raincoat was about to bite into one when Demetrius broke a piece off, without asking, and began to devour it.

''Elp yerself,' said Raincoat, pushing the plate over to him. '*Mia casa, tua casa.* '

Demetrius chomped away. I had to intervene.

'Is that what I think it is?' I asked Raincoat. He nodded. I told Demetrius it was a hash cake and he shouldn't eat any more, as he'd never taken a psychoactive drug in his life.

'Tastes fine to me,' said Demetrius, gorging himself. Whether out of bravado or sheer greed he polished the cake off. 'I'll see you all later. I'm off to – er – look at the Rembrandts.'

Demetrius viewed museums as 'the graveyards of culture – wouldn't be seen dead in one.' I knew he was off to peruse some life studies of a more exotic nature.

Pandemonium. Raincoat and I got back to the Museumzicht, our small hotel with the eternal stairs, a couple of hours later, to find a doctor at Demetrius's bedside, administering intravenous valium.

Demetrius grabbed hold of the doctor's arm. 'I'm dying,' he said in a state of total panic. 'I'm dying.'

'No, you're not,' said the doctor, 'you're just hysterical.' He unloaded the valium into Demetrius's arm.

The sedative began to work and the doctor left. As soon as

he was out of the door Nico came in, wafting great clouds of incense over Demetrius, followed by Wadada playing Fauré's *Requiem*.

'Oh God! Oh God!' cried Demetrius, horrified at the apparition of Nico hovering over him. 'Get away! Get away! The Angel of Death . . . Get away!'

Demetrius was never really the same after that. His old anxious, misplaced self returned to claim him. The inhaler and the Bullworker became his constant companions again. They say that travel broadens the mind. Demetrius's mind had been stretched to places it didn't want to go. Out-of-body experiences, feelings of absurdity, paranoia, anxiety.

'I genuinely thought I was going mad,' he said later. 'Apparently ingesting hashish is five times more powerful than smoking it . . . I'd never even had a puff of a joint before.'

He rested up at the hotel for a few days. Occasionally he'd venture outside. I'd find him standing in the middle of the road, peering through an imaginary sextant.

'Perceptual distortion,' he'd say. 'Perceptual distortion.'

Then he moved to another hotel, taking the tour float with him. There, he entertained everyone with a curious charade, claiming that his room had been burgled and the money stolen. We called the police. They knew the hotel well, a perfectly straight establishment with a desk clerk and doorman. Demetrius, however, seemed anything but straight to them. According to the desk clerk he'd filled his room with a bevy of Thai callgirls, so it was easy to work out where the money had gone.

Then Demetrius left. Just disappeared.

Angel 666, Barcelona (Homage to Catatonia)

Nico, Eric Random and I had been having a disorientating time of it down the Ramblas, tripping over jugglers and bumping into mime artists. There was no room for honest scum anywhere. Eric thought he knew the way back to the hotel, so Nico and I doggedly followed him, keeping our eyes fixed firmly on his brand new, calf-length, black, Spanish *bootees* (size 7, ladies). One blind and black alleyway looks much the same as another in the Gothic Quarter and within minutes we were lost.

Having paid a kid to lead us out of the barrio, we arrived at the venue — Club 666 — to find ourselves enigmatically billed as 'Nico and the Hasidim'. The mystery was solved, however, when who should walk on stage in the middle of the performance, but Dr Demetrius himself, dress as Hasidic rabbi, in long black overcoat the hat, brandishing a copy of the Bible.

'The Angel of Death. The Angel of Death,' he kept repeating. The audience was completely mystified. We carried on playing, like it was part of the show. Nico didn't notice him, until he was standing up against her, staring manically.

'The Angel of Death.'

'What are *yooooo* doooing here?' Nico asked.

Demetrius just stood there, impassively staring.

'Get out! . . . Go!'

He didn't move.

She shoved him.

He swayed a little, but remained rooted to the spot.

We turned up the volume and blasted him off.

Then he showed up again the next day at a live TV date: *The Angel Cassas Show*. It was in a variety theatre. A traditional sloping stage, footlights, individual dressing-rooms, the works. The stall seats had been removed and tables and chairs put in their place, so it would resemble a cabaret. The audience sat eating and drinking, while the host, Angel Cassas himself, smoothly compered an eclectic show that consisted of topless dancers, James Burke (the communicator), a Rumba troupe, and Nico. Demetrius was still carrying his Bible, and now wearing a crucifix as well as the Hassidic gear.

Nico was anxious about Demetrius's craziness, whether he was going to pull another stunt like the night before. He was hanging around outside her dressing-room, pacing the corridor, reading aloud apocryphal passages from the *Book of Revelations*.

Eric Random and I sniffed about the Bluebell Girls. Though they were a permanent feature of the Angel Cassas show, half of them came from Blackburn. They had long fantails of pink ostrich feathers, worn over a sequined G-string, and up top nothing but pert, powdered, pink titties and smiles as wide and eyes as blue as an empty sky. One of them plucked a tail feather and gave it to Random. I asked him if I could borrow his Tantric talisman to see if I had any luck.

'This 'asn't left my neck since I was in Nepal,' he said in a hushed, reverential voice. 'It was blessed by Baba Yoni 'imself.'

We were on after the girls. Angel Cassas was giving mouth, some silky-slick patter to the middle-aged punters, getting them horny. Then Nico was supposed to come on and sing her *saeta* of woe.

Cue. Camera. No Nico.

We had to start playing, so we did a long intro . . . then a verse . . . but still no Nico. A third of the way through the song, we heard the clump and jangle of her boots. She stomped on stage, furious. Strangely, her dressing-room intercom had been switched off. The audience started tittering. I looked up at the backstage balcony: there was Demetrius, *eating* his Bible. We finished the song, the clap man signalled the audience to applaud. Above the polite patter, Demetrius could be heard admonishing us all to 'beware the Angel of Death.' This caused some offence to the management as they thought Demetrius was referring to Angel Cassas. I managed to calm them down, explaining that Nico's manager was undergoing some sort of spiritual crisis and had been this way for weeks.

In all this hysteria, Nico seemed to have become strangely steady. An atmosphere of insanity seemed conducive to her sense of well-being. It made her feel normal. She was now just another person in the bus. And that's the way she liked it. That's who she was. One of the boys.

Digital Delight/Ringfinger Surprise

Beating the borders was always a challenge. Various subterfuges were employed as we crisscrossed our way across fortress Europe. Nico would adopt the disguise of a prim librarian – specs, hair in a bun – but unfortunately it was undermined by the black leather trousers, the biker boots and the leather bracelet with silver skulls. And, as her eyesight was perfect, the alien lenses distorted her vision so much that she could barely discern a familiar face, let alone the inquisitorial stares of officialdom.

Customs officials, it has to be said, ain't the brightest of individuals. They always pull the brokendown old 2CVs with brokendown hippies inside, or the conspicuously guilty pop group with the pills and potions in their underpants. Meanwhile the professional hustler in the black BMW with a briefcase full of cocaine is waved on through. This prejudice infuriated Nico, to the point where she would become contemptuous of even her own fear. Once, as we were driving off the car ferry at Dover, she handed me a bunch of used syringes, a whole tour's worth. I quickly threw them off the ramp and into the oily black water below, thanking her profusely for the macabre bouquet.

Nico's preferred method of concealment was to buy a pack of condoms (a source of great embarrassment to her: 'I'm sure they must think I'm a hooker when I buy these things') and a jar of vaseline. Then she'd fill the prophylactic with a clingfilmed ball of heroin. This she would insert into her behind, generally about five minutes from the border. This is how it would go:

'Are we ne-ar the booorder?' We'd heard it sung so many times it had become a familiar refrain along with 'Have you got a little bit of haa-aash?' Out would come the condom, a look of disgust on her face. Then she'd wriggle out of her leathers. Everyone would suddenly busy themselves with displacement activities: books that hadn't been opened throughout the tour would suddenly become intensely fascinating.

There's a particular customs post north of Lille, on the French/Belgian border, every time . . . every single time. . .

Demetrius was whistling inanely a nerveless, tuneless ditty of his own making.

'We're a touring party of jazz musicians . . . we have a carnet . . . I am Miss Paffgen's personal physician . . .' It was never any use. They pulled the bus apart, seats upturned, instruments out of the cases, dirty laundry everywhere. Then the pockets – we lined up one by one, emptying our pathetic secrets on to the desk. The chief poked through the pile, saying nothing, nose twitching above his black moustache. You could picture him at home, a photo of Jean-Marie Le Pen on the dressing-table; humping his wife while she picked spinach from her teeth.

We knew what was in store, it was ritualistic and we were resigned. They probably knew it was a waste of time, but that's what they were there in the world to do – waste our time.

One by one we were led off to the 'interview room'. Nico banging into things, blind as a bat (the glasses had to go).

A thin little guy with rat eyes asks me to undress. He inspects each garment, examining the lining. Then he holds my arms under a lamp to check for needle marks. On the table lies a pair of surgical gloves and a tube of lubricating jelly. If you piss these guys off you don't get the jelly. There's a knock at the door. A female officer is standing there, a small bull dyke with cropped hair and a big black gunbelt. She's excited, they've found something.

Back in the chief's office, I ask Eric Random if he got the finger.

'Yeh,' his eyes lowered. 'Creep asked if 'e could 'ave me phone number afterwards.'

Nico comes in with the dyke, looking suitably crushed and repentant.

The chief starts typing out a charge: possession of prohibited substances and unpaid debt. The central Paris computer has thrown up some ancient hospital bill Nico hasn't paid.

They got what they wanted. A token. Nico had stashed a shot's worth of dope in her knickers (the rest of the stuff still safely concealed in its traditional hiding place). They were happy with that. A few smiles, a few jokes. Demetrius resumed his whistling.

Fear is always a problem of scale.

Brixton

''Im aint naw docturr!' Mrs Chin blocked the top of the stairs to our flat. 'An' *she* aint naw music teacher neither.'

Dr Demetrius
Nico
Me
Random
Instruments
Luggage
Boxes of unsold Nico T-shirts
Bullworker

'An' 'im,' she pointed to me, ''im naw in the middle ages . . . An' 'oo be 'e?' She pointed to the svelte figure of Eric Random. 'What 'as bin goin' on in this 'ere 'ouse aint nawbady's bisness . . . like a 'erd o' buffalo, up an' down dese steers . . . Amma feart a knock on mi own door fer t'look inside . . . blood! Blood on de walls!'

Mrs Chin had got into the flat while we were away. Clarke and Echo had been in permanent residence, contributing their unique refinements to our Brixton salon. Needle orgies every night. The place looked like it had been gangbanged.

Echo and Clarke crept in later, after Mrs Chin had shaken the rest of us for the rent and given us our notice to quit. Needless to say, Bertie and Jeeves hadn't paid a penny towards the upkeep of the place. The phone was off – red bills of over £500 to Dr Mengele threatening disconnection. Demetrius's annoyance was tempered by the thought that not only did the evil doctor of Auschwitz have Mossad on his trail, but he would also have to answer to British Telecom as well.

*

Clarke and Echo had been to Australia together for a couple of weeks. Echo spelt out the hazards to me as Nico was to do the same tour imminently. He told me how the promoter had personally threatened him, accusing him of being a parasite on Clarke. Nico said, 'You two should get married – I guess for them it's like you're living in sin.'

Any hints of homosexuality threw them both into a stir of Catholic homophobia. 'It sez in the Bible,' etc etc. In fact, for Clarke, mentioning any kind of male sexuality risked an unwanted reference to the seat of shame itself: 'the three-piece suite, the sausage and mash – God's cruellest joke.'

Echo reached in his jacket pocket and pulled out a couple of snapshots. One was of a girl who looked like Alice in Wonderland but with an Edgar Allen Poe twist, an emaciated child-woman who looked like she'd scratched her way out of a coffin. 'Met 'er in Sydney, wonderful girl, 'Elena, amazin' 'ow she's kept 'erself tergether – yer'd never guess she was on the gear would yer?' He showed me his other snap. 'They 'ave whales up near Brisbane,' he said with awe. I looked at the photo, it was a picture of the empty sea, nothing else.

'But where are the whales?' I asked.

'They dived,' he said, pointing to a blank area of sea. 'But that's where they were. '

Echo complained of a perpetual toothache but said he couldn't go to the dentist as he was scared of injections. Also he'd told Dr Strang back in Prestwich hospital that he was 'sick of the bloody methadone . . . I want what they give prisoners – bromide. Ev'ry time I get the bus up ter Prestwich I get a fookin' 'ard-on cos o' the vibrations . . . the only way I can ged it down is ter think o' the bleedin' dentist. '

You'd get dizzy listening to Echo's explanations of his life. Sooner or later he'd get round to how disloyal I'd been not quitting Nico's ensemble when he did.

'But you didn't quit,' I said, 'you were fired.'

'Yeh, but I wouldn't 'ave bin if you'd quit too, then it would 'ave bin proper workers' solidarity.'

'Workers? Nico and Demetrius fired you because you're a

junkie,' I said. 'She's not your mother . . . she doesn't need dependants, she's got her own habit to look after.'

'But after all I fookin' did fer 'er . . . an' fer you.'

Nico was also turning weirder by the minute. One day I caught her rifling through my coat pockets, probably in search of cigs or a bit of change. The kleptomania reached its peak when I found out she'd pinched a love-letter of mine from Norway.

'It wasn't very interesting,' she said, 'the usual gerrl's stuff.'

'That's all right, then,' I replied, 'just pass on the bills as usual.'

We had a red-hot row about it that became really childish. She started off with all that nymphomaniac stuff again so I called her a nosy old nun.

'Can I have it back?' I demanded.

'I've lost it,' she said.

I grabbed her shoulder bag and rummaged inside . . . God, the junk in there, something from every hotel of every tour, packets of soap and shampoo (never to be used), stationery, an ashtray . . . but no letter.

'You see, I'm telling the truth,' she said. 'I've lost it . . . so you can believe me when I tell you it's not worth reading.'

It was always the same old junkie meta-logic. Any nonsense could be justified, any absurdity rationalised.

Demetrius had also had enough, retreating to Manchester to recuperate. He had to find another road manager in his stead, someone dependable and unbreakable. Raincoat pleaded for the job, but after the poisoning attempt Raincoat's days were numbered. Besides, Raincoat was doing a new Frankie impersonation – the Man With the Golden Arm – for real. Raincoat had joined up with the Undead and was now plying his mission on the street. Demetrius felt there was no alternative but to bring in a character he'd threatened us with before – the Big Grief.

> We-e-e-ll . . . 'ere we are
> 'n 'ere we go 'n geddawayeeay
> . . .Rockin' all over the world.

'C'mon, let's fookin' 'ear yer! Sing up! That means you, snoggin' each other in the back . . . Now, are yer right, Nico? 'Ave yer got yer words sorted, luv? Sound. Right, I'll count ter four an' then all tergether . . .'

Grief was the last in a long line of missing links, Cro-Magnon throwbacks from Eccles. Demetrius had pulled him in to control us and to punish us. Eccles is a social anthropologist's paradise, the sinkhole of Manchester, where the indigenous troglodytic inhabitants have squatted round campfires, roasting carcasses and molesting each other's wives for millennia. Now their caves all have satellite dishes but their table manners remain the same. Grief was indigenous Eccles. Hair a long frizzy helmet, huge canine teeth and an expression of permanent rabid rage. He'd learned his craft down the Stretford End, cracking skulls, throwing (and catching) Irish grenades, potatoes with razorblades stuck in their sides. Grief was playtime dread, everything you ever feared back in the schoolyard.

'Right! One more time! . . . Just listen ter Nico – singin' 'er 'eart out, arntyer luv? An' they lost the fookin' war! So, come on, loud an' clear . . . 'Rockin' All Over the World' *one more time*!'

DOWN UNDER NICO

Dennis picked us up at Sydney Airport in a Rolls. He'd hired it just for the trip into town. He wanted to spoil us because it was in his nature – he had this good feeling about us. Late forties, stocky, tough, he was the Boss of the Job in Sydney. He knew every angle, every crack behind the wallpaper. His girlfriend ran a chain of high-class brothels called That Touch of Venus. Venus had many moons, one of which was a mobile bordello in a converted trailer, lined with pink fur, called Transports of Delight.

'When we started out t'gither, Venus told me I couldn't fack 'er . . . straight up, said I'd 'ave t' wait til the wedding night – but I could 'ave it on the 'ouse till then . . . wadda woman.'

'A goddess,' I said

He dropped us at the Cosmopolitan Hotel at Bondi.

'Anythin' y'want – come t'me. Any problems – come t'me.'

'We want ter go to That Touch of Venus,' said Random.

We went to the beach instead, where we immediately fell asleep, dreaming of Venus and catching sunstroke. That night we both had a fever. Then the next day our skins started to fall off in great patches. 'Enough to make a lampshade,' said Nico. It looked like she'd brought a couple of lepers along with her when we did our first date at the Piggery in Byron Bay.

The Piggery was a converted abattoir, if you could call it a conversion; basically they'd just slaughtered all the pigs. It still stank of pigshit and animal fear. It was a deeply inauspicious place to start a tour. The Piggery audience were expecting to hear a hugely popular local support group called the Headless Chickens, but they got killed in a road smash on the way to the gig. There was an atmosphere of sadness and latent anger, as if we were somehow responsible. The Curse of Nico.

Everywhere we went, we bombed. It just wasn't their thing: like California before, they danced to a different beat, theirs being essentially garage rock – lots of grungy guitars, fast and funny lyrics, walloping drums – no poetry, it just makes you feel good. Nico's ship of doom had definitely docked into the wrong port. For the first time, though, she was philosophical about it. She knew her stuff was an alien brew and it didn't hurt her too deeply, it didn't feel like total failure. Though Dennis's 'good feeling' about us had rapidly degenerated into acid indigestion he still remained charming and encouraging. He genuinely adored Nico, wanted to protect her. She was a real lady, she had '*class*, mate'. He knew all about Nico's habit and it concerned him, even hurt him, to see her mistreat herself like that – but he'd been around enough to know that there were no quick cures or clever explanations. He liked us all, even Grief. When Dennis told us the girls at That Touch of Venus had all been trained in the arts of love by a Thai sex guru, Random's talisman started to twinkle. We kept bugging him for an intro. It was only fifty yards up the hill from his own club. The girls lived in. We'd see them drinking coffee and hanging up their smalls in the laundry room as we passed by, to while away the afternoon in Dennis's office, while Nico followed the white rabbit through Wonderland with Echo's girl, Helena.

Helena was indeed Echo's anima, his feminine counterpart. Thin and wasted, obsessed with heroin and its whole history, she would hold seminars. Did we know, for instance, that Bayer, the company that first manufactured aspirin, also came up with the first synthesised Diacetylmorphine and that they patented it under the name 'Heroin', as a cough cure? That was back in 1898. Did we also know that it was legal for nearly twenty years? We didn't. She offered everyone a sample and then went into a detailed description of the physiological and neurological effects as they occurred. Did we know that opiate molecules attach themselves to certain receptor sites in the brain? We didn't. The high being the act of making these neurological connections, and that the opiate molecules imitate the action of endorphins, which are the body's natural analgesic? We didn't.

'Weird ter think of all them endolphins swimmin' about in yer brain, in't it?' said Toby.

Bondi offered Nico most of her everyday needs – all-night pharmacists and healthfood shops. Nico was on something of a health kick at the time. She'd settle on one food substance – like yoghurt – and she'd stick exclusively to it. The idea of planning a menu for herself and then eating it alone was too depressing a prospect. So she'd just think *yoghurt*. You don't need to chew yoghurt.

At first it seemed the gigs would do well in Sydney. The first night they packed the place and the reviews were on our side. But Dennis had booked Nico in for three shows. There just weren't enough doom-dwellers in Paddington and Bayswater. Junkies there might be aplenty, but the difference was the sun shone all day on their craniums, all that melanin produced wallflowers who needed a different aesthetic climate to Nico's teutonic fog.

On days off Grief would herd us into the bus and insist we explore the hinterlands. 'Gerraway from all this faggot 'ealth food and microbiotic bollox.' He took us up into the Blue Mountains, where great flocks of parrots would break their roosts high up in the trees and dive and circle above our heads. He made us *walk* – something we'd grown unaccustomed to.

Most of the time Nico had to stay behind to do endless interviews. Dennis had tried every promotional angle. TV, radio, newspapers. But still the attendance at shows was little more than a dribble.

Nico's connection in New Zealand was arrested before we arrived and he'd given her name to the customs.

'They even squeezed out my toothpaste,' she said. Luckily she'd handed her stuff to Toby in the arrival lounge and he did the lot on the spot.

At the Glue Pot in Auckland (the name gives some hint of the clientele – mostly high on solvents) there was a bevy of separatist dykes standing at the front, keeping up a nonstop chant the moment Random, Toby and I stepped on stage. 'We want Nico – we don't want you! We want Nico – we don't want you!' Whenever there was a lull in a song they'd stick their noses into a cellophane carrier-bag, get a head full of Araldite, and start up again. During a break between numbers I whispered to Nico to tell them to shut it.

'He says,' she said, pointing me out to our chorus of superglue valkyries, 'tell the dykes to shut it.'

After the show they came hunting for me backstage and I had to be escorted from the building for my own safety.

The local promoter said he'd taped the show and thought it might make an interesting live album.

'With all that heckling?' I asked.

'Especially with the heckling,' he said. 'Novelty market, mate.'

Did I have any ideas for a title?

'How about *Down Under Nico*?'

Back in Oz, our four nights in Melbourne coincided with the Australian leg of Bob Dylan's endless world tour.

'I'd so like to see Bawb . . . it's been such a long time.'

Dennis called Dylan's tour management. He got the classic rock 'n' roll runaround . . . call back at such and such a time, maybe you will, maybe you won't. Finally Dennis got 'Maybe Bob will drop in and see Nico after his own show.'

Nico was so excited, like it was a date. She had a bath and bought a new shirt. Throughout the gig she kept craning her neck, scanning the audience for a glimpse of Lonesome Bob. When he didn't show I found her crying in the dressing-room.

'No one comes to see me any more.'

One late afternoon back in Bondi I bumped into her on the street. I was carrying bottles of sunscreen for me and Random and she had her daily carton of yoghurt. She seemed uncharacteristically cheerful, so I said why don't we go down to the sea? She said she couldn't swim.

'How's about a paddle?' I suggested.

'OK.'

We rolled up our trousers and walked along the shoreline, still carrying our groceries. I reminded her of a heckler from the Brisbane show: 'Doncha know no happy songs, darlin?' She giggled, then started singing 'Daisy, Daisy, give me your answer do'.

'I bet that's the first English song you ever learnt,' I said.

She just smiled and carried on singing, swishing her feet in the water, happy in the sunset.

After the Canberra show, in search of something to do in Australia's eerie Brasilia, Toby, Random and I phoned up for three hookers. 'Yew in a greup, theen?' said mine, already looking at her watch. 'First off – I don't swallow it, noway. Even with me boyfriend I always spit 'n' rinse after with List'rine.'

The bumps and grinds, sighs and moans, started up in the rooms on either side of mine. She wasn't bad looking, just lacking any pretence of sensuality.

'Fancy a cup of tea?' I asked.

'If y'like.'

She checked her wristwatch again. After precisely one hour she banged on the wall.

'Right then! Finish 'em off, girls!'

Later we three clients sat around talking about Nico, a subject perfectly suited to post-coital *tristesse*. We all seemed to have come to the same conclusion, separately, that Nico's need for heroin far outweighed any other ambition she might have. We knew that, ultimately, anything we might contribute musically was incidental. If we wanted to be either serious or indifferent then it was our own affair. Despite *Camera Obscura*'s enthusiastic reception, and the resurgence of interest in her, Nico remained a slave to her habit. Japan was the last leg of the tour, and then we agreed it would be time to take our leave of Estradella and her Dog of Doom.

Before we left Australia Nico met a biker in Perth called Squasher. He had a Harley and plenty of what Nico liked.

'Him big fella,' said Random, looking like a streak of black ink beside Squasher in conventional biker mode of sweatstained T-shirt and arse-crack jeans. Squasher would bring Random bags of fresh marijuana heads and take Nico off for long rides along the coast of the Indian Ocean to see the 'dawlphins'.

For some time after Nico would refer nostalgically to her Knight on the shining Harley. 'Squorscher . . . I miss him soooo.'

Squasher was the only guy I ever heard her sound really fond of. He had no sophistication or artistic pretensions, no misguided romantic yearnings for *La Belle Dame Sans Merci*, and no camp illusions about the Moon Goddess. He was just a regular guy and Nico could be his regular girl if she wanted.

'Just hop on the back, darlin, wrap yer arms around me barrel and let's kick-start each other t' heaven.'

WHAT A LITTLE MONEY CAN DO

I wanted to get something out of the last few shows with Nico.

I recalled Demetrius's weird appearance on-stage in Barcelona. When it came to the last number in the set I'd disappear, don a black coat and hat, grab a broom and come back on as a street sweeper. I'd sweep up, over Toby and Random, brushing the dust off them, brushing Toby's drum kit and interfering with his playing. I'd brush the baby talc off Random's tablas, finally ending up with Nico. I'd hobble around her while she sang Jim Morrison's 'The End', then I'd shoot her with a toy pistol and she'd collapse on to the harmonium. ('Don't yer know – only a silver bullet will finish the job,' mocked Random.)

The Italians loved it, the more lunacy on stage the better. Nico and I began to ham it up so much we started to look forward to showtime. At one show I got the support group to bring me in on a bier. On another occasion we accompanied Nico on the first tune, twanging rubber bands. Real amateur-night stuff. The more ludicrous we made it, the more involved the audience became; the more we hammed it up, the more seriously they took it.

The Japanese weren't so sure, at first, about the weirdness. They'd come to see a dignified, creative presence; Nico was an art object to them, like Van Gogh's 'Sunflowers'. You paid your money and you stared. I'd creep around the stage in my overcoat and hat with a flashlight. Nico would wail about her dead dreams, Random might be combing his hair or reading a newspaper. The punters didn't know what the fuck was happening. Strangely, though, it wasn't just a put-on; for once, we were trying to do something – trying to be entertaining.

Though I'd told Nico I wanted to leave, she seemed to have forgotten. When the time came and she realised I wouldn't be doing her next tour she told Demetrius, 'Just put him in the vaaan.'

On the quiet, Demetrius had taken a tape of some of our live work to a record company, located in a unit on an industrial estate somewhere in South London. The stuff had been taped off the mixing-desk without any live atmosphere and thus it was only the ghost of what a live performance could be. Plus it had been recorded on to the cheapest cassettes available. It was never intended for anything other than self-reference. Demetrius got £4,000 for it and Nico suddenly found herself with a new album called *Nico: Behind the Iron Curtain*. Actually it was recorded in a punk club near Rotterdam.

Then Demetrius got Nico fixed up with a tour of Northern Greece, crazy stuff. Random put his Bedlamites back together, all ten of them, and off they went with Demetrius and Nico for £15 a night each and a chance to play their own stuff as support. They were young Didsbury jazzers and they wanted to blow all night long. Nico, to them, was just a washed-up old relic from a bygone era.

When Warhol died Demetrius fixed up a memorial show in Brixton, a tacky piece of opportunism for Warholics Anonymous, with a couple of Andy's riveting home-movies and a disorientated Nico playing with a curried jazz backing, Indian ragas and funk riffs. It was back to nowhere again for the Pop Girl of '66.

Then, after a year of playing tavernas and village halls she offered me another tour of Japan . . . £100 a night. The only drawback being that she had to share the bill with John Cale.

*

I'd hardly seen her for the best part of a year, and there was a distinct change in her. She looked older but seemed happier. She was tired of the endless tours and now just wanted to do the occasional well-paid prestigious show. She seemed less burdened than before; though we'd have the usual after-dinner conversations about death, mortality and decay, it was in a lighter vein. She'd quit heroin and was now on the methadone programme instead. To get high she'd smoke pot and to calm down she'd drink alcohol.

(After Toby and I, the last of Nico's original brood, had left, Demetrius had desperately wanted to get back on to the Sunshine Tour bus. Nico's habit had proved to be a grotesque liability. All those crazy scenes and outrageous compulsions. If she had a methadone script it would make her easier to handle, more docile, and there would no longer be the constant anxiety over whether she was about to run out.)

Nico seemed to be more secure about herself and clearer about what she wanted to do in the future – stop touring, write her autobiography and drop Demetrius.

'I think it's time, no? It's not that I hate him or anything, but these tours, carrying all these people around, I'm so tired of all that. It's not going anywhere. Time for something else, something new.'

Nico thinking of the future? Glimpses of a serenity beyond despair?

We were talking about death, as you do after a good spaghetti dinner.

'I've got so close to it, so many times . . . it's like you begin to see it. First, when you're young, it doesn't exist. Then later it's a shadow, indistinct. Then you begin to recognise it as it gets closer . . .'

Though she'd been intimate with the deaths of others – her father, murdered by the Nazis; her mother's death of cancer in a mental asylum; the execution of the American sergeant who'd raped her; the gravedust-laden air of Berlin – she'd also monitored her own mortality in her songs and in her life. Other people's deaths are not the same as your own.

March '88:
THE PINK & THE BLACK

As you head into Tokyo from Narita Airport, you become immediately aware of Tokyo heading towards you. The ever-expanding ingenuity of the city ensures that its dreams are kept within easy reach. On the left, King Ludwig of Bavaria's castle replicated in superstone and plexiglass for Disneyworld; Love Hotels, fantasy sex palaces with heart-shaped jacuzzis and '64 Cadillac Coupe de Ville-shaped beds. *Pinkku*. The ultimate, coveted, erotic dream icon for the Japanese male is the delicate pink underflesh of a virgin's inner labia. *Pinkku*. For the Japanese as a whole, the precise moment of the highest erotic arousal occurs at the second before loss of innocence. Love Hotels help to maintain that highly-charged adolescent atmosphere . . . besides, domestic accommodation is frequently so cramped that couples are often obliged to conduct their entire sex lives in such places.

The traffic slowed to a near-stop. Beyond the Love Hotels and the cathedrals of kitsch was the dirty Sea of Japan, fizzing with a constant rain. Yuki, our interpreter, apologised for the traffic congestion. A truck had gone off the road and smashed into the lane barrier. As we passed we could see directly into the cabin – the driver slumped dead in his seatbelt, the rain beating down on his steaming truck.

The Ropongi Prince Hotel is built like a Pavlova cake with, as its featured centre, a glass-sided heated pool. It cost £20 a splash. There were no takers. We had a pre-tour conference with the management team to discuss the stage set-up, sound, lighting and so on. Nico was tired and absented herself but Cale, always concerned with the minutiae of performance, was as punctual as ever. I hadn't seen him much in the past couple of years and I was surprised at the transformation. Indeed the new slimline, calorie-controlled, alcohol-free, no chemical additives, one hundred per cent pure Caleness came as something of a shock to us all. He just didn't seem like the flatulent Druid we'd known from before, who drank champagne from a pint mug. He must have lost four stone at least, and looked ten years younger and fitter. His hair was dyed a very fetching purple/black and cut in a Rosa Klebb crop. He exuded health – and wealth. Did I want to come and look at some clothes at Issey Miyake's? No thanks. I had about £10 in my pocket, and until after the first show it was staying there. Did I want to go for a wander round the Shibuya stores? No.

The cherry trees were in blossom and the promoters suggested we go and sit under 'the chelly brossom' for good luck.

We went for a walk in Yoyogi Park – Nico, Cale, me, Dids, Grief and a young guitar-player called Henry. Henry was very keen, very capable – but totally inexperienced in the ways of Nico. He was never quite sure which image to adopt. He had on a pair of Chinese slippers, camouflage trousers, black polo neck, green leather Gestapo coat, blue eyeliner and a Nero haircut topped with a black beret, circa 1958 Left Bank Paris. His broken nose gave him an air of toughness that was undermined by a public schoolboy nervousness. Girls were a source of inner panic and perplexity to Henry. He'd blush if introduced to one. Grief suggested a trip to a No-Panties bar, where the floors are mirrored. Henry reflected but didn't understand. When Grief explained, Henry was horrified. He was a *vegetarian*.

Every Sunday at Yoyogi Park there's an amateur talent show. Down a long avenue there are groups lined up, all playing at once. It's a living Rock 'n' Roll Museum. There must have been a dozen Elvises and five or six Beatles, even three diminutive, slightly tubby girls miming to the Supremes. The further down the avenue we went the more esoteric the acts became, until we got to the Japanese Velvet Underground.

> A *wa kassu sha da po ga weh*
> To *ar tomaros patees?*

Though Cale looked a lot younger and more closely resembled the man of his Velvet Underground days, he was concealed beneath a large beaver fur hat and a cashmere overcoat; and Nico was hardly her old physical self. The Velveteens didn't recognise their role-models staring them in the face.

Nico and Cale were not getting on well. He objected to her smoking in his presence. Then there were problems about the shows; Nico wanted to go on last; 'This John Cale – who does he think he is? I'm a star too.' But Cale was top of the bill. Though he'd been booked to play with a group he'd turned up on his own at the end of a long solo tour. The Japanese were politely astonished at such a blatant breach of contract.

His act was so sharp and synchronised that he didn't want the stage cluttered up with Dids's old car parts and he insisted on the piano being tuned after I'd used it. Nevertheless his contract stipulated a group, so he had the idea that Dids, Henry and I should round off the evening with him doing a karaoke medley of Velvet Underground hits.

'I'm not exactly *au fait* with the Velvet Underground material,' said Henry. 'What do you think I should do?'

'Just turn your amp up to ten,' I said, 'and look like you don't care.'

Nico didn't like the idea of us playing with Cale, it made her feel more marginal, more of a warm-up act. So on the way to every show there were rows about who was doing what, and the order of appearance, and the fact that Cale absolutely refused to perform a number with Nico.

'Oh go on,' I said. 'It'd be like Sonny and Cher getting back together again.'

Cale always sat in the front passenger seat, the Demetrius seat, taking in every inch of the city space. 'This is the future,' he'd say, pointing out a feature of some building none of us could see because his hat blocked the view.

'Johnny Vi-o-la! Johnny Vi-o-la!'

Cale ignored her. Nico sat behind him, pointing and snickering at the beaver hat and rubbing her fingers together to suggest Cale's moneyed status.

Johnny Vi - o - la Johnny Vi - o - la

It took on a singing, chant-like quality. 'So fashionable now, so chic . . . such a transformaaation.' She whispered in my ear, 'But still a schmuck,' and enshrouded him in a cloud of Marlboro smoke.

Typically, we were inadequately rehearsed, our raggedness emphasised by Cale's streamlined performance. Dids was deep into his hubcap metal-bashing. You'd hear a conventional drum pattern, then suddenly there'd come this clanking of ghostly chains that threw the rest of us completely. Dids would peer out crossly at us from behind a canopy of broken cymbals and twisted metal, shaking his head and admonishing us before the assembled audience.

Cale, by contrast, sprang on to the stage and straight into his repertoire, barely pausing between songs. You'd hear him in his dressing-room, practising right up to the last minute some tricky little guitar figure. Alone with his piano or a simple guitar accompaniment, he personified total confidence and mastery of his material. He seemed to have got his act under control at last

– the bellicose self-indulgence burnt out earlier in the day on the squash court.

As the tour progressed Cale distanced himself further and further from the drifting derelicts of his past. Every day he'd work out on the squash court: super-concentrated, super-confident, for the evening's work ahead.

We took the bullet train to Osaka. Cale refused to sit with Nico and me. He thought smokers should wear plague bells. I had alcohol poisoning from a misguided attempt to outdrink Grief in a sake bar the night before. Cale was delighted, it meant he could crow, as the freshly converted do, about the merits of clean living.

At the evening meal he enthused about the sushi. 'Mmmm – this raw dolphin is re-a-lly de-e-licious . . . want a slice, James?'

(At an earlier gastronomic encounter the waitress brought a bowl of clear broth to the table, then added a few vegetables and some prawns. We assumed the prawns were dead, but one of them leapt out of the boiling liquid. The waitress held it under with a pair of chopsticks. Nico fled outside to throw up.)

After the Osaka show an angel stood outside Cale's dressing-room, clutching an exquisitely wrapped parcel. Cale was her personal god. But, like a lot of gods, he was hard to get in touch with, and had insisted on a dressing-room at the opposite end of the corridor from Nico and her etceteras. He did *not* wish to be distracted from his purity of purpose by anyone. I recalled Raincoat's dictum of yesteryear, 'It's only pop.' On behalf of our Nico-tine-stained retinue I demanded admittance.

'The girl's been waiting all her life,' I explained. 'She's got type-outs of all your lyrics. She's more than a fan, she's a true believer.' I gained an audience for the trembling disciple.

The girl is shy, word-panicked, mute. Her eyes glance briefly at the face of the slimmed-down bard of the three-minute-forty-second psychodrama, then down to the floor again in *sonkei* (respect). She has a specially-prepared speech she'd like to make, if possible.

'Yes, yes, yes. Get on with it,' says Cale.

The girl reads from her notes: 'John Cale. I thank you for your beautiful music. Please accept this gift in sincere appreciation of your gift.'

Once more her gaze tentatively touches the image of the performer-priest-king, before being lowered again in veneration.

Cale takes the parcel, snatches at the butterfly-ribboned bow and tears open the lovingly-wrapped package. Inside the silk-lined box is a porcelain presentation bottle of vintage sake, in the shape of a Kabuki demon mask. Fierce red eyes, diabolical black beard, death-white skin. Grotesquely beautiful and stunningly expensive.

'I don't drink,' says Cale, and hands the flask of demon alcohol back to her.

The girl puts her humble offering for the god down on the altar of his guitar-case and leaves in tears.

Osaka star dressing-room
Girl cries
Cherry blossom falls.

Hotel Osaka Grand

Late afternoon. Upper-class schoolgirls, thoroughbred daughters of Mr Sony and Mr Mitsubishi cycling across the bridge in dark navy sailor tops, long pleated skirts and smog-masks.

At night you enter a forest of neon, there are no addresses and no sensible way of finding anywhere, even the neon is transient. Architecture as advertising space.

Cale: 'When you're playing Northern California they come up to you out of the past and say, "Remember that blowjob I gave you in 'Frisco in '67?" What are you supposed to say? What do they want?'

On the TV there are constant newsflashes about a teenage pop-star's suicide. Close-ups of the Tokyo hotel window she jumped from and the bloodstained ground she pulped on. She'd been dropped by her record company on her seventeenth birthday, *because* she was seventeen. So she dropped herself. The boys back in Artist & Repertoire want the quintessence of adolescence, 13–16, after that the *Pinkku*'s all used up.

Back at the Ropongi Prince in Tokyo the pool just steamed, all by itself, lifeless and empty. Cale wouldn't because he was too tight, and Nico couldn't because she didn't swim. Then a bunch of guys arrived from George Michael's TRUE FAITH world tour – they were all wearing identical leather flying jackets, emblazoned with George the Greek's tour logo. G.M. himself was staying at the Tokyo Hilton, away from prying paparazzi, in his own private floating world of geisha satori. Soon his minions were splashing about in the pool. 'More health freaks,' said Nico.

Crowds are different in Japan, they're more self-controlled. Coming out of the Shibuya subway the traffic stops for the crowds to cross the square from all sides, in perfect black and white symmetry, like an Op Art kaleidoscope. Then it's the traffic's turn. While you're waiting to cross, high above the square a giant video advertising screen, the size of a tennis court, sells you pieces of techno heaven. There's no such thing as dead time in Tokyo. As you walk up the hill towards Parco, the crowds don't saunter untidily as in the West, but seem organised by a hidden common purpose. No one touches, but all are linked by an invisible thread of meaning. Roundeyes walks alone.

The last show was in the Seibu Theatre in the Parco store complex. Somewhat akin to having the Wigmore Hall in the middle of Harrods. The Japanese are a little more honest about these matters than we are and see no contradiction between art and commerce.

Cale complained that we had to share a dressing-room. Immediately a no-smoking zone came into being. The shows were early and he wanted to go on first in order to do some last-minute shopping.

Dids, Henry and I did the Velvet Underground stuff with

him, came off, and then went on again to do Nico's set. Our reappearance took the wind out of Nico's sails and the polite, but lifeless, applause at the end left her despondent. Compared with her last tour of Japan, which had been successful both in audience rapport and in financial terms, this was a half-hearted affair. They'd seen Nico the year before, but this was Cale's first trip to Japan and so there was more of a novelty value attached to his appearances. Novelty is intrinsic to success in Japan.

'Famous not popular,' was the verdict on Nico from Mr Hidaka, Yuki's boss.

As for Cale, Yuki advised us to come to some financial agreement with him, as he'd been paid for a group and we'd accompanied him on every show.

'Let's have a breakfast meeting and discuss it then,' said Cale, hurrying off to thread up at Yamamoto.

I booked an alarm call for 9.00 a.m. and made it to the coffee and bun for the first time in a while. Henry and Dids were waiting, scowling.

'Am I late?' I asked.

'Ow yez. You might as well 'ave stayed in bayed,' said Dids. 'Cant's done a runner!'

'Yes,' said Henry, 'I think it's jolly bad form.'

Cale had taken the six-o'clock morning flight out, to the surprise of the fastidiously polite, quietly furious promoters. Yuki was astonished at such peremptory rudeness.

On the way to Narita Airport Nico rummaged inside her bag.

'Look! John left me a present . . . and I thought he hated me.'

She opened the parcel. Why, it was a presentation bottle of vintage sake in the shape of a Kabuki demon mask.

'Jesus . . .' She recoiled in disgust. 'It's horrible.'

She passed the bad magic on to Grief, who drank the lot down.

'I'm never sharing a bill with that aaasshole again!'

*

Wrong. Three weeks later she had to share a double bill with the tightest coracle in rock 'n' roll at the Palais des Beaux Arts, Brussels. The show had been booked by Demetrius.

Demetrius had turned up with the whole of Didsbury, in the shape of Eric Random and his Bedlamites, who thought they were the star turn. Nico, Dids, Henry and I had flown in earlier.

'I've brought along my fellow free spirits who wish to share the camaraderie of the open road.' Demetrius was in a semi-ecstatic state.

He'd just come out of hospital after two months' incapacitation due to a broken leg. He'd jumped off a garage roof. No one knew exactly why he'd climbed up there in the first place. There was talk that his unrequited love for Nico had finally driven him over the edge. There was also the suggestion that the good Doctor had become involved in certain curious nocturnal practices. His demeanour was certainly different. He now walked with a limp and carried a stick, which he jabbed at the ground to underline his pronouncements.

'I have knelt before the shining gates of Heaven, and I have crawled beneath the gaping jaws of Hell . . . and believe me, James, though, in truth, we live upon a dungheap covered in flies, I draw comfort from the close consolation of the human reek.'

Everyone wanted to play, but Dr Demetrius's circus of free spirits wouldn't fit on to the stage. Random was sulking and combing his hair furiously. He'd missed out on Japan, having been there the first time round. In Tokyo were his chosen handmaidens, awaiting their annual dose of Tantric Love Juice.

Cale had checked himself into a separate hotel and had ensured that he was given a private dressing-room in another part of the theatre building. 'He thinks he's Von Karajan,' said Nico. 'More cheese sandwiches for us,' said Demetrius.

Nico and I did a version of 'My Funny Valentine' which, apart from that time in the Signora's basement, was probably the best we could ever do with that song. We just emptied it out into a bare piano waltz for the emotionally crippled.

Amazingly, Cale allowed Nico to duet with him on one of his songs, a setting of Dylan Thomas's *A Child's Christmas in*

Wales. Nico fluffed her lines halfway through, blushed and went shy, but he prompted and carried her to the end, bringing the show to a rapturous close. Later he did his usual disappearing trick and vanished to his hotel the moment he was paid.

Back at our hotel in the Place Roger, Random and I noticed a furtive Dr Demetrius hobbling off down the street. At that time of night, and in the teeming rain, he could only be up to one thing. We followed him. Round the block was a whole street of bordellos. Demetrius was window shopping. He stopped outside one, peered momentarily inside to check the merchandise, then pressed the bell. A few minutes later Random and I followed his example and slipped discreetly into the red velvet night.

LOST IN THE STARS

Nico's attic flat, perched high above Prestwich, was immaculately tidy. She sat crosslegged on the bed, typewriter at her knees, working on her autobiography, her life and her house in order. Once a week she'd nip to the local chemist to get her methadone prescription filled and pop it in her bicycle basket along with her groceries, like a Gothic *hausfrau*. But she still disturbed the neighbours. Though she smiled now as she chatted about the pleasures of cycling and the benefits of a healthy diet, the silver skulls on her black leather bracelet, the small ivory death's-head hanging from her neck and the ineradicable needle scars all over her hands and arms suggested a less conventional history.

The relentless desire for self-degradation had abated and the all-enshrouding cloak of her addiction had lifted. She was now the middle-aged spinster lady who lived next door, the one with the interesting past.

Although Demetrius had found Nico the flat and had got her on to the methadone programme, now that she was tidying everything up she felt his substantial frame took up an unnecessary amount of room in her life. Though her existence appeared outwardly normal Nico remained devoid of conventional notions of loyalty. Friendship, in the traditional sense, imposed too much upon her privacy. There were those, however, who remained steadfastly loyal to her, despite her lack of sentimentality.

Lutz Ulbrich had been Nico's companion from '74 to '78,

when they lived together in the Chelsea Hotel. He'd accompanied her on guitar at her concerts throughout that period. It was also at this time that she'd become addicted to heroin. Lutz chose to break free of the drug scene and so they split up. He became an independent musician, involved in performance projects in Berlin. One such project was a music festival called Fata Morgana he was organising at the Berlin Planetarium. He commissioned Nico to perform a specially written piece and suggested that she do it in tandem with me.

Demetrius still saw himself as Nico's manager, but unfortunately Nico didn't, and she saw no reason why she should pay him a percentage of an independent commission.

My phone never stopped ringing with accusations from Demetrius of disloyalty and subterfuge, but I kept reminding myself of the 'missing millions' from his *Behind the Iron Curtain* neo-bootleg. I was just pleased that my fee had suddenly increased from £100 to £300.

As ever, Nico only had a few sketches, so we recruited Henry and Dids to lend substance. Nico grew bored with even the idea of a rehearsal and so we were left working much of it out in the sound-check.

Without Demetrius and the old team there, the whole thing assumed an air of workmanlike quasi-professionalism, something I'd only experienced before in Japan, but without its dazzling disorientation. In other words – dull.

Nico's new positivism also implied a more self-conscious awareness of the music and it affected me to the degree that, for the first time in a long while, we were both paralysed with stage-fright.

'I think I'm going to have a heart attaack,' she said.

Our nerves weren't helped by the fact that the dressing-room was in an annexe of the main Planetarium building. We had to climb out of a back window, through a fire exit and then walk down a corridor which ran round the building's circumference. We spun on to the stage.

There were two shows. The first was an audience victory. What's great and terrible about the Germans is that they believe in what they do, even when they're just listening. We were unnerved and outfaced. Because the building was a dome the sound kept whirling round the walls so everything would get repeated by a delayed echo. I didn't know who was playing, me or my shadow.

By the second show we'd figured out the way from the dressing-room. We turned up the volume and gave it a go. The Planetarium people switched on the universe and we all got cosmic. It wobbled out of time and Nico wailed out of tune and the asteroid showers could be a little disconcerting, nevertheless the audience could tell we were giving it our best shot.

They demanded an encore. Nico asked me what I wanted to hear and she sang my favourite of all her songs,

> When I remember what to say
> When I remember what to say
> You will know me again
>
> You do not seem to be listening
> You do not seem to be listening
> The high tide is taking everything
> And you forget to answer.
>
> ('You Forget to Answer')

It was the last song she ever performed.

THE HOT CLUB

Someone dies and you immediately start to flick back through the snaps. Hunting down the clues. The last time you saw that person on the step of an Italian restaurant in Berlin. The last embrace.

I thought she'd see us all out. Tougher than the leather of her boots. I could see her at eighty, a terrifying old bat in a black cloak, swooping down on her latest victim.

Demetrius called me to say Nico had died while on holiday in Ibiza. She'd fallen off her bike, he didn't know the details.

The funeral would be in Berlin. Lutz Ulbrich would arrange to have Nico's body flown from Ibiza to Berlin, where she would be cremated. He'd found an entry in her diary which said, 'I want to be burnt,' next to a handwritten copy of Blake's 'The Tyger'.

Demetrius felt it was an injustice to bury her ashes in Berlin, when she'd expressed a desire for her remains to be buried on the moors above Manchester. He had a pal, Mike, who was the vicar of a church up there. Mike was neither a pious cleric nor some trendy priest with an electric guitar. He looked more like a stonemason, with his beard and craggy hands – you could picture him heaving granite blocks into place on a drystone wall, rather than reading the lesson in front of a threadbare congregation of high Tory matriarchs.

Demetrius really wanted his own Nico wake. He was her manager, he'd handled her career for the past seven years, so he'd choreograph her funeral. He informed the *Melody Maker* that there would be a memorial service for a grieving nation up at Mike's church. There, Demetrius read poetry to a captive congregation of me, Eric Random, a couple of Goths and a fellwalker in an anorak and bobble-hat.

While I was up in Manchester I called in on Echo to gauge his reactions to Nico's death. He now lived in a house divided between saints and sinners. He and Clarke lived in the front room while Faith and the children occupied the rest of the flat. Echo had brought all his bric-à-brac in there with him – the Venus of the Fireplace, the broken guitars and religious ephemera. He lay on his sofa wrapped in a blanket, angry that Demetrius had only just informed him of Nico's death with a curt and anonymous note through the door, saying merely, 'C. Paffgen, deceased 18/7/88.' He also resented Demetrius for having encouraged Nico to go on the methadone programme.

'She might 'ave bin 'appier, but it still killed 'er when she came off the gear. 'Appens all the time ter junkies, the scag keeps yer young, makes yer 'air look nice 'n' shiny.'

Echo's reasoning remained centred around heroin.

'It keeps yer under control . . . y'know, the sex business. If yer need ter fuck then yer'll never be 'appy. Yer see, Jim, women're above us, they 'ave ter be. Yer've got yer 'Oly Family, then yer saints 'n' angels, an then yer've got women takin' care of it all down 'ere. They're the 'ighest form of life. So what we do to 'em as geezers 'as got ter be beastly, ant it? Nico knew all about that first 'and, an' she wanted out of it. If yer take gear then all the guilt just disappears.' He snapped his fingers. 'Yer don't 'ave ter *want* or *remember*. An' yer learn ter treat women with the respect they deserve.'

He propped himself up on the sofa, pulled the door open slightly and shouted down the hall. 'Purra brew on, pet!'

Funeral No. 2 was a couple of weeks later in Berlin. Demetrius was still perturbed by the idea that Nico's ashes would not be interred up at Preacher Mike's place, so I suggested we should take a raw stone from up on the hills as her memorial. We got the rock and lugged it back to Manchester to find that it didn't conform to the German *Verordnung*, so Demetrius had to commission an expensive, correctly proportioned and racially pure one from a funerary mason in Berlin.

We set off for Berlin in a Mercedes tour bus with videos and reclining seats. On board were me, Demetrius, Eric Random, Dids, Le Kid, Preacher Mike and a blues singer from Oldham called Victor Brox. Victor had brought with him bags of 5p pieces, which he was going to use on German cigarette machines. He had a long mandarin beard with beads threaded in it. He liked a decent pint, a nice piece of ass and a good fart. Amazingly, it was Victor Brox who, hanging out in Ibiza in the early sixties, had first encouraged Nico to sing.

'I can't work out whether the world owes him a debt, or he owes us one,' said Demetrius, irritated by the delays at every German truckstop while Victor pumped the ciggie machines with 5ps. Herr Bluesmeister Brox quickly got the nickname from Demetrius of 'Hans Off' (as in 'Hands off cocks – it's Victor Brox!')

Though it was a funeral party it still had the feeling and approach of a rock and roll tour: there remained a steady smog of hash smoke around Eric Random, and Preacher Mike happily shared the whisky bottle, letting Demetrius wear his dog-collar. Demetrius picked up his customary bumper set of porno-mags along the autobahn; even Le Kid seemed content, still trying to stick together that eternal jointlette.

However many times we'd made that trip down the corridor to Berlin the sensation was always that of entering a walled city-state. (How often had we driven past the same sentry posts, the same flyblown cafeteria, serving the same flyblown East German food; the same Russian tank atop its memorial column supposedly the first to liberate the city in '45?) It stopped the city from becoming just another Euro-metropolis for steel-eyed techno-Teutons. All the kids who were dodging military service found a refuge there in Kreuzberg and formed the core of Nico's audience.

'With how many eyes does a man enter a city . . .' said Demetrius as we bought our visas. 'In search of the unseen, the perfect memory, the moment set apart from all other moments when a place, a gesture, a woman's smile, will assume a permanent significance in his heart?'

Travel narrows the mind – rock and roll tours especially, vacuum-packed to keep out ordinary reality. Demetrius had a love affair with the road itself, with change as the sole constant in his life, protected from the unwarranted incursion of the unknown upon his nervous sensibility by the company of his conscripted pals. They provided the steady temperature and environment for him to make the occasional probe into alien soil.

'. . . And the businessman flying into Berlin or New York – what does he seek or expect? Is he, when he phones for a callgirl, or just chats up a colleague's secretary, is he also trying to let the memory take root?'

Victor Brox answered him: 'We-e-ll a city is like a worman/ you godda find a way to her heart/ah sayed – a city is la-a-ke a worman . . .'

16/8/88 Berlin

It was a lovely day for a funeral. Bright blue sky, temperature in the eighties. The Grünewald-Forst cemetery was at the edge of the woods, out by the Wannsee, the lake which provides Berlin with a seaside, where folks go sailing and skinnydipping in the summer. (And where, at the Wannsee Conference in January 1942, Reynard Heydrich first presented the detailed plans for the Final Solution.)

It was an intimate setting, the smell of evergreens and aromatic shrubs hanging in the still morning air. A quiet oasis away from crazy, overheated Berlin.

The memorial stone Demetrius had ordered wasn't ready, so there was just a small marker, a spike with a disc on top which said, 'Paffgen 16.10.38 – 18.7.88'. The hole was about half a metre square and a metre deep. Demetrius limped over, still using his walking-stick, one leg now shorter than the other. Random and Dids were behind a hedge, pulling things out of their pockets. Preacher Mike called everyone together.

'Not where she wanted to be,' muttered Demetrius.

'She wasn't all there anyway,' said Random.

'She's not all there now,' I said. 'The best average is only twenty-five per cent of the loved one's ashes actually getting into the urn . . . they don't rake out the grate every time.'

'James, old boy,' said Demetrius, 'I would remind you that this *is* a funeral.'

Le Kid appeared with the urn in one hand and a ghetto-blaster in the other. Preacher Mike said a few words from the *Bhagavad Gita* – he'd met Nico and knew what she was about, so there was no pretence of piety. Then Le Kid placed the urn in the ground, rested the cassette-player at the mouth of the grave, and switched on. It was a recording of Nico singing 'Mütterlein':

> *Liebes kleines Mütterlein*
> *Nun darf ich endlich bei Dir sein*
> *Die Sehnsucht und die Einsamkeit*
> *Erlösen sich in Seeligkeit.*

> (Dear little mother
> At last I can be with you
> Longing and loneliness
> Are redeemed by inner peace.)

As soon as the harmonium started up, that was enough for Demetrius, and he staggered off, pale and trembling, into the bushes, inhaler at the ready.

A few people had come on their own, like Philippe Garrel, the film director, the only man Nico said she'd ever loved. A shy, rumpled little guy in a borrowed suit and tie, he'd made the effort to get there from Paris.

After the ceremony we all joined up for a few drinks in a lakeside café. Nico's auntie Helma bought the drinks and told us how pretty 'little Christa' was as a child, how she was always with her mother and that it was good she was buried beside her. Dids said he'd seen a little shrew jump out of the grave during the service. Demetrius remarked upon the absence in any form of the New York contingent.

'That Garrel's a decent sort – came all the way on his own from Paris. But that New York lot . . . not even a bunch of flowers or a message.'

'Too Cool,' I said.

'I hate Cool,' he answered. 'Cool is when you're dead.'

That evening there was a memorial concert back at the Planetarium. Lutz had organised it as a means of paying the funeral expenses. Everyone did a turn – Victor Brox warmed things up with a Death-Rattle Boogie. Then they played a recording of Nico's last concert which had taken place in the same building, and switched on the stars and whirling planets. Again, at the sound of Nico's disembodied voice, Demetrius fled. I also left the weird necrophiliac rite and went to the dressing-room where I found Lutz and a bottle of Jameson's. He told me what had happened in Ibiza:

'After the Planetarium concert Nico went to Ibiza. I'd planned to join her, but I was worried about all the hash-smoking. Eventually I decided to go but the night I packed my bags Ari (Le Kid) phoned to tell me Nico was dead. So then I don't know what I should do. I still decide to go, as Ari needed help to fix the funeral.'

I asked Lutz how she died.

'She'd been renting a farmhouse in the woods. She and Ari had been arguing . . . she wanted to go off and buy some hash. It was the middle of the day, and she put on a turban because she had a headache. A witness said he'd seen her on her bike in good shape then, five minutes later, further on down the road, she was lying in the middle of the sidewalk. She couldn't speak or move down one side. The guy didn't know what to do. He flagged a cab to take her to hospital. As soon as she heard the word 'hospital' she waved her arm to say 'no'. The cab didn't want to take her anyway, but the guy persuaded him. Then she was taken to a hospital, but they didn't have any doctors. So they went to another – the same story. Then they got her to the big hospital. On the stretcher she was still waving her arm. She had an operation and they found blood on the brain. Nobody knew who she was. She was just some old junkie. The next day

Ari wondered where she was and called the police. They had Nico's description and told him to go to the Cannes Nisto hospital. When he got there he found she'd died in the night. The terrible look on her face of . . .'

Lutz paused to find the right word, '. . . *aloneness.*'

Next morning I went for a meeting with the promoters of the Planetarium concert to discuss what should be done with the live recording of Nico's last show, which now belonged to the Berlin City Council. Just before the meeting began Le Kid announced that he had something important to say. More eulogies perhaps? He poked around inside his carrier-bag and produced two large medicine bottles that had belonged to his mother.

'Ees zere anyone eere 'oo would lak to buy some mezzadone?'

You can't help admiring someone who cuts the crap and gets straight down to business. And Le Kid had been doing good business the past couple of days – what with the memorial concert (the proceeds of which Demetrius had assumed would go towards the funeral expenses, but which instead went straight into Le Kid's wallet), and now Nico's unused cache of methadone, Le Kid was mopping up.

'Muz be werf two gees, easy,' he said, smiling. 'I can do eet for a good price.'

We declined Le Kid's offer, and discussed what should be done with the live recording. Le Kid was insistent that Nico's estate (i.e. Le Kid) should get all the publishing, so there was an initial impasse. Since it had been more of a collective effort than a solo one, I felt the musicians should get a percentage of any royalties which might accrue from a future record release. A 60/40 split was agreed, in his favour.

(Later, Le Kid gave a cassette copy of the Planetarium concert to a character in L.A. called Joe Julian. He'd done a bit of studio work with Nico earlier in the decade and had a copy of Nico's out-takes in his possession. Together with the material from the live concert – with judicious fades where applause begins – he managed to persuade Enigma Records that he had some original Nico music 'produced' by himself. They gave him a pleasant purse and put out a tacky piece of merchandise called *Hanging Gardens*, which was described on the sleeve as 'Nico's last studio recordings'. Neither Le Kid nor anyone else, except Joe Julian, ever saw a penny from this unfortunate, yet predictable, postscript to Nico's career.)

After the meeting we left Le Kid behind to blow the dough, packed Nico's few belongings – the harmonium and her bag of clothes – into the bus, and headed home.

'I say, chaps,' said Demetrius suddenly during a lull in the journey, 'don't let's have any tasteless confessionals appearing in print, in the form of "My Life with Nico" or "The Last of the Bohemians", or any other such opportunistic banalities.'

Absolutely. We all agreed.

'Of course,' he added, 'for a man of acute literary sensibility, like myself, such a subject would lie beneath my concern.'

As we came into France, north of Lille, our favourite customs post gave us the traditional shakedown. Demetrius immediately broke into his nervous whistle.

Waiting for us in the shed was the same rodent-eyed little 'flic' who'd finger-fucked Eric Random the last time we dropped in for a tête-à-tête.

Everyone had to wait by their personal luggage while Rateyes's pals combed the van. A sad little shoulder bag, with two empty motorbike boots standing to attention on top, remained unclaimed in the corner. Rateyes asked us who it belonged to. Demetrius spoke up:

'You may recall the last time we visited your establishment. We had with us a singer, a good German lady by the name of Fraulein Paffgen. I was her personal physician. It is with great regret that I must inform you that she succumbed to an accident while on holiday . . . fell off her bicycle . . . Sadly she is no longer with us.'

'So where ees she now?'

'Above or below – who can say? Beyond the comprehension of mere mortals . . .'

Rateyes's whiskers twitched.

'Dead,' said Eric Random, getting to the point.

Rateyes still wanted to sniff inside her bag. He motioned Eric to bring it to him.

'An what ees ze style of musique zat you play?' He spread Nico's belongings over the counter.

'Pop,'/'Jazz,' said Demetrius and Eric simultaneously.

'Jazz,' repeated Eric, throwing Demetrius a black look, 'definitely jazz.'

Rateyes fingered a pair of Nico's grey knickers. 'Aaah . . . *J'adore le jazz* . . . Django Reinhardt, Stéphane Grappelli . . . You like ze 'Ot Club de Paris?' he asked.

'Never bin,' said Eric.

NICO DISCOGRAPHY

The Marble Index (Elektra) 1969
Desertshore (Warner Brothers) 1970
The End (Island) 1974
Drama of Exile (Aura) 1981
Live in Denmark (VU) 1983
Camera Obscura (Beggars' Banquet) 1985
Behind The Iron Curtain (Dojo) 1986